Revelation

Volume 1

by

Paul M. Sadler, D.D.

Revelation

Volume 1

by

Paul M. Sadler, D.D.

President of the *Berean Bible Society*

Author of:
Exploring the Unsearchable Riches of Christ
The Life and Letters of the Apostle Peter
The Triumph of His Grace
Studies in James
And other Bible Studies

BEREAN BIBLE SOCIETY
N112 W17761 Mequon Road
PO Box 756
Germantown, WI 53022
(*Metro Milwaukee*)

First Printing 2012

Library of Congress Catalog in Publication Data
Sadler, Paul M.
Revelation, Volume 1
Includes bibliographical references and index
ISBN 978-1-893874-39-8
1. Bible. 2. Grace (Theology). 3. Bible Teaching. 4. Title.

All Scripture quotations are from the *"The Old Scofield Reference Bible"* 1909, 1917, 1937, 1945 by Oxford University Press, Inc.
—King James Version

Cover art: ©iStockphoto.com/Viktoria Makarova

Printed in the United States of America

WORZALLA PUBLISHING COMPANY
STEVENS POINT, WISCONSIN

Contents

In Grateful Appreciation 9

Introduction 11

1. *The Beginning of the End*

   Grace and Peace • Which Coming? • A Journey
   Through Time • The Two Witnesses 19

2. *The Judge of All the Earth*

   The Seven Golden Candlesticks and the
   Son of Man • Preparation for Battle •
   Fear Not! • The Apostle's Commission
   to Write • A Word to the Wise Is Sufficient 39

3. *The Kingdom Church at Ephesus and Smyrna*

   The Jewish Assembly at Ephesus •
   Angels in Church • The Kingdom Gospel •
   The Paradise of God • The Jewish Assembly
   at Smyrna • Trusting God in Trying Times •
   Martyrdom 55

4. *The Kingdom Church at Pergamos and Thyatira*

   The Jewish Assembly at Pergamos •
   The Throne of Satan • The Danger of
   Compromise • The Rewards of Obedience •
   Something to Think About! • The Jewish
   Assembly at Thyatira • The Conflict of the Ages 77

5. *The Kingdom Church at Sardis and
   Philadelphia (Part 1)*

   The Jewish Assembly at Sardis •
   Watching and Waiting • The Jewish
   Assembly at Philadelphia 101

6. *The Kingdom Church at Philadelphia (Part 2) and Laodicea*

The Hour of Temptation • The Reward
of the Inheritance • A Practical Note •
The Jewish Assembly at Laodicea •
Indecision • An Honest Evaluation •
In Summary 117

7. *The Throne Room of God*

Setting the Record Straight • A Scene
that Defies Explanation • Who Are the
Twenty-Four Elders? • The Four Beasts •
He Who Is Worthy of Worship 135

8. *Worthy Is the Lamb*

The Book Within the Book • A Declaration
of Worthiness • A New Song •
Two Amazing Doxologies 153

9. *The Four Horsemen of the Apocalypse*

First Seal—The Rider of the White Horse •
Second Seal—The Rider of the Red Horse •
Third Seal—The Rider of the Black Horse •
Fourth Seal—The Rider of the Pale Horse 171

10. *The Wrath of God*

Fifth Seal—The Avenger of Blood •
The Sixth Seal—Signs of the Times •
Understanding the Times • The True
Nature of the Last Days of Grace 185

Endnotes 199

Selected Bibliography 203

Dedication

This book is affectionately dedicated to my beloved wife, whose unfailing support has been one of the inspirations of my ministry.

IN GRATEFUL APPRECIATION

To God the Father of our Lord Jesus Christ who gave me this opportunity to share what lies ahead, in what is commonly known as *things to come*.

To all those who prayed for and sacrificially contributed to this project that others might come into a fuller understanding of the Word, rightly divided.

To Christine Mulholland, our in-house artist, who selected the picture for the front cover and put the finishing touches on art work.

To my dear wife, Vicki, who smoothed out the rough spots in the manuscript and proofread it with patient perseverance.

To Nicky Brillowski and Kevin Sadler, who masterfully laid out and typeset the entire volume. Kevin also offered many helpful suggestions.

To my colleagues Ricky Kurth, Alan Neubauer, and Don Weffald who systematically proofread the whole manuscript with an analytical eye. Their recommendations and constructive criticisms were invaluable. As the Scriptures say, "Iron sharpeneth iron; so a man sharpeneth the countenance of his friend," and that was certainly true in this case.

It is the author's earnest prayer that this volume will give the reader a greater appreciation of the grace of God under which we are currently living. May it be used of the Lord to help you grow in the grace and knowledge of our Lord Jesus Christ. AMEN!

INTRODUCTION

I have been reading some of the journals of Meriwether Lewis and William Clark and I must say it's a remarkable account of courage. In 1803, President Jefferson commissioned Lewis and Clark to explore what we now know as the Pacific Northwest, shortly after the *Louisiana Purchase* from France. It took them approximately a year to acquire the necessary supplies and put together the forty-member expedition. Every member of the team was the best of the best in his particular field, and for good reason.

On May 14, 1804, the expedition left St. Louis, traveling northward through South Dakota into south central North Dakota where they spent the winter. This was the farthest west that any white man had ever journeyed. On April 3rd the following spring, Lewis and Clark led the expedition westward into Montana, uncertain of what they would face as they resumed their journey into the great *unknown!*

The fear of the unknown can be unsettling. We believe this is especially true of the unbeliever who senses the world is on the eve of destruction, but doesn't realize the seriousness of his unsaved condition. Since these things are spiritually discerned, we bear the responsibility to warn men everywhere to flee the wrath to come. Paul himself reasoned with Felix regarding righteousness, temperance, and the **judgment to come** (Acts 24:25).

The love of God sent His dear Son to the Cross that we might enjoy a knowledge of sins forgiven and deliverance from the day of His vengeance. But if the salvation which is in Christ Jesus is rejected, God will someday pour out the fierceness of His wrath upon the unbeliever. Before we can effectively warn men, we ourselves must first be equipped with a better understanding of *things to come*. This is why it is essential to proclaim the whole counsel of God, which includes the Book of Revelation. Of course, we must always do so in light of Paul's letters to the Church the Body of Christ, where we are instructed to rightly divide the Word of truth. This will help us to distinguish between the last days of Israel and the last days of grace.

THREE IMPORTANT KEYS

A key gives access—that is, of course, if it's the right key! The same is true regarding spiritual things. There are three important keys that unlock the complexities of the Book of Revelation.

First, it is essential to have a well-rounded knowledge of the prophetic Scriptures, which unfold God's purpose for the earth. The Book of Revelation is merely a *continuation*, the further development and capstone of prophecy. We should understand this when we read, "Blessed is he that readeth, and they that hear the words of this *prophecy*" (Rev. 1:3).

It has been correctly said that the fruits of Revelation are found in the roots of prophecy. We believe the best commentary on the Bible is the Bible itself. The Scriptures interpret themselves if we leave them as God gave them to us. Remarkably, most of the symbolism in the Book of Revelation that has been a stumbling block to many is explained in other portions of the Word of God. Sometimes it is defined in the Apocalypse itself. It is important to bear in mind that the term, Apocalypse is a synonym for the Book of Revelation.

For example, John saw the Son of Man standing in the midst of seven golden candlesticks (lampstands), holding seven stars in His right hand. We are thankful not to be left to our own imaginations as to the proper interpretation. The seven golden lampstands are seven churches in Asia and the seven stars are seven angels (Gr. *aggelos*), or messengers of these seven assemblies (Rev. 1:20). As you can see, the symbolism in the book gives way to a *literal* interpretation when we compare spiritual things with spiritual things.

The Book of Revelation plays a very important role in prophecy, simply because it gives us a chronological order of future events not found in the Old Testament or the four Gospels. John, under the direction of the Spirit, gathers up all these Old Testament prophecies concerning things to come and places them into a time sequence which shows the reader when each prophetic event will be fulfilled. He then gives us important connecting *links* never before revealed. We know, for example, the Kingdom was foretold by the prophets David and Daniel, but John is the first to reveal that the duration of it would be 1,000 years (Rev. 20:4).

Although John digresses here and there, Chapters 1 through 10 primarily address the first three and one-half years of Jacob's Trouble. With so many events unfolding in the middle of the Tribulation period, he spends the better part of four chapters (11-14) describing the ramifications of the Abomination of Desolation. In Chapters 15 through 19, John deals extensively with the horrors of the Great Tribulation, which is brought to a close by the Second Coming of Christ. Then in Chapter 20, the apostle dramatically draws back the curtain on the Great White Throne Judgment, followed by the eternal state on earth in Chapters 21 and 22.

Second, it is essential that we also have a proper understanding of Paul's apostleship and message. Failure to do so will only serve to frustrate the grace of God. Clearly, the

Mystery program of God is disconnected from the future prophecies of the coming Day of the Lord. We are living in God's *unprophesied* Age of Grace. This is why every attempt to predict the Rapture of the Church based on a prophetic timeline has failed.

Probably some will read this next statement in disbelief, but it is nevertheless true if we understand Paul's gospel: No Old Testament prophecy is being fulfilled today. We agree that the world is heading in that direction, and even would go as far as to say the stage is being set. But wisdom says we must stop here for this reason: After the Rapture, once the prophetic clock re-starts, numerous prophesies will be fulfilled in rapid succession because they are all *interrelated*. Here's a case in point: The prophecy that the Anti-Christ will stand up in the Temple and declare himself to be God is dependent upon the fulfillment of a foregoing prophecy that the Temple will be rebuilt. You see, the fulfillment of one event is dependent upon another.

Since we have escaped the wrath to come, it was not needful for Paul to instruct the members of the Body of Christ to heed the warnings found in the Olivet Discourse or the Book of Revelation. The Rapture is an *unprophesied* event; therefore, there are no signs, times, or seasons that have to happen before the Lord's imminent catching up of the Church. Little wonder that the apostle says to those at Thessalonica, "Comfort one another with these words" (I Thess. 4:18). Paul would have never made this statement if we were going through any part of the coming Tribulation. This helps clarify why the Body of Christ is never mentioned in the Book of Revelation.

Third, we must adopt the correct theological viewpoint for an accurate interpretation. The *preterist view* says the

Book of Revelation is only written about the problems and persecutions of the early Church which existed at the time of the writing. That is to say, all the events of Revelation have already occurred! This view defies reason, logic, and most importantly, any credible evidence.

The *historical view* says that the record symbolically describes the chronological sequence of historic events in the Church. A modified form of this position states that the seven churches in Asia represent seven historical stages of the Church, the Body of Christ. According to this view, we are currently living in the Laodicean age. While this is perhaps the most popular position among dispensationalists, it too leaves much to be desired. The problem here is that we are left with man's interpretation of Church History, which itself is questionable at times. We prefer to leave the final authority in such matters with the Scriptures themselves. Furthermore, the Body of Christ is not found in prophecy and, as such is not described or chronicled in the first three chapters of the prophetic Book of Revelation.

There is one view which we believe aligns itself perfectly with the Word of God. With the Lord's help, we will share this position with you in our comments on Chapter 1.

It is generally agreed that the Apostle John wrote the *Book of Revelation* around 96 A.D., which historically seems to be the case. Prof. Charles R. Erdman, D.D., made the following insightful observation as to whether John was banished to the isle of Patmos under the reign of Nero or Domitian.

"Historians agree that the Neronian persecution hardly extended beyond the city of Rome, while the persecution under Domitian was spread widely over the empire. The persecution under Nero was not on the grounds of religious belief.

He wished to avert from himself suspicion of the crime of having burned the city [Rome], and therefore attempted to implicate the new sect called 'Christians.' This was in A.D. 64, and there is no proof that his fiendish cruelties to the infant Church continued until or during the year A.D. 68.

"On the contrary, the martyrdoms under Domitian were due to a refusal on the part of Christians to worship the emperor as divine....The ground of persecution, therefore, indicates the reign of Domitian and not that of Nero. Nor did the means of punishment adopted by Nero include banishment. There was imprisonment, torture, drenching with oil and then burning the wretched victims as torches, and crucifixion; but exile is not mentioned. On the other hand, there are detailed stories and references to a general policy of banishment as employed by Domitian."[1]

The Church Fathers also confirm that John was banished to the isle of Patmos under the reign of Domitian in 96 A.D., the same year he would have received the Apocalypse. This would mean that the vast majority of the Kingdom saints, including John's fellow apostles of the Kingdom, had already preceded him in death. Paul, too, had passed from the scene, having suffered martyrdom at the hand of Nero. Furthermore, the Temple in Jerusalem would have been destroyed by Titus in 70 A.D., which essentially ended Judaism.

Although men speak of the end of the world in terms of a nuclear holocaust, worldwide pandemic, or an asteroid hitting the earth, the fact of the matter is that God will have the final word in the affairs of His creation, as clearly foretold in the Book of Revelation. He is sovereign! As Daniel writes, "He doeth according to His will in the army of heaven, and among the inhabitants of the earth: and none can stay His hand, or say unto Him, What doest thou?" (Dan. 4:35).

But some question, if God is in control, then why does He seemingly allow evil to prevail in the world? Brethren, today God is not charging men with their sins; rather, He is giving them every opportunity to believe the gospel. That's grace! This does not mean He has forgotten their unrighteous ways, as the events of the coming Tribulation demonstrate. Mark these words and mark them well: The unbeliever who *rejects* the gospel is storing up the wrath of God against himself. A record of his sins is being kept "against the day of wrath and revelation of the righteous judgment of God" (Rom. 2:5 cf. II Cor. 5:19).

—Paul M. Sadler, D.D.

Milwaukee, Wisconsin
January 12, 2012

1

The Beginning of the End

> "The Revelation of Jesus Christ, which God gave
> unto Him, to show unto His servants things which
> must shortly come to pass; and He sent and signified it
> by His angel unto His servant John: Who bare record of
> the Word of God, and of the testimony of Jesus Christ,
> and of all things that he saw."
>
> —*Revelation 1:1,2*

The world has always had an insatiable desire to know the future. Even Hollywood has sought to capitalize on this with movies like *Back to the Future*. With man's fallen nature, you can be certain that if he were able to predict the future it would be for evil purposes. We are thankful that God has hidden all future events from mankind, except for those He has chosen to reveal to us concerning things to come, which are spiritually discerned. Only the Word of God gives us an accurate account of future events; all other sources are the devices of Satan. As we are about to see, an understanding of the Book of Revelation re-shapes our worldview entirely.

With God's help, we plan to present a birds-eye view of what lies ahead, commonly known as the Day of the Lord. The purpose of Volume One of this commentary is to dispel the notion that the Church, the Body of Christ is the subject of the first four chapters of the Book of Revelation. We will also be exploring the coming events of the Tribulation to further our appreciation of the grace of God. Having a better understanding of these matters will cause us to bow our knee in humble adoration to the One who has promised us deliverance from the wrath to come (I Thes. 5:9).

The consensus among Bible teachers is that the Book of Revelation is a sealed book that cannot possibly be interpreted accurately due to the nature of the numerous visions and symbolic language. Consequently, those who desire to study this prophetic account are discouraged from doing so since they've been told it cannot be understood. This, of course, is unsound reasoning for the very first verse teaches otherwise:

> "The Revelation of Jesus Christ, which God gave unto Him, to show unto His servants things which must shortly come to pass; and He sent and signified it by His angel unto His servant John" (Rev. 1:1).

The revelation (Gr. *apokalupsis*) spoken of here is from Jesus Christ according to God's prophetic program. Unlike the four Gospels, where Christ is portrayed as the lowly suffering servant, in the apocalypse, He is presented as the Judge of all the earth, prepared to pour out His wrath upon His enemies. This is the revelation that was *shown* to His servants that must soon come to pass. It is noteworthy that the Apostle John will closely adhere to this theme throughout the book.

Of course, this revelation must be distinguished from the one the Apostle Paul received. He says concerning his gospel: "For I neither received it of man, neither was I taught it, but by the revelation of Jesus Christ" (Gal. 1:12). The revelation (Gr. *apokalupsis*) given to Paul from Christ is in accordance to the Mystery, which has to do with our exaltation with Him in the heavenlies. Today, we know Christ as the God of all grace who has declared a cease-fire with this Christ-rejecting world. As a result, *amnesty* is being offered to all those who will trust Him as their Savior. But God's declaration of grace and peace will soon give way to a declaration of war, as the Book of Revelation plainly sets forth. Whatsoever God has separated, let no man join together; thus, it is essential that Paul's and John's revelations of Christ are not intermingled in a misguided attempt to harmonize them.

While the various theological positions that were presented in the Introduction have been weighed in the balance and found wanting, we believe the *futuristic view* aligns itself more closely with John's visions in the Spirit. This view holds that the *entire* Book of Revelation is futuristic. One thing in favor of this position is that both biblical history and the Scriptures clearly support it.

It is generally accepted that the Apostle John wrote the Book of Revelation around 96 A.D., at the age of 90. (This shows us that we are never too old to be used of the Lord.) Archbishop James Ussher (1581-1656 A.D.), who developed the dating system that appears in most reference Bibles, concurs. He was one of the first to date the books of holy Scripture by meticulously comparing both secular and biblical documents at his disposal, many of which no longer exist.

By the time John wrote the Apocalypse, the blessing of God had completely departed from Israel. The Temple and Jerusalem had already been destroyed by Titus, the Roman conqueror; consequently the sacrificial system lay in ruin. Both Paul and Peter had suffered martyrdom, and the majority of those saved at Pentecost under the Kingdom gospel were with the Lord. This raises the question: To whom, then, was John writing? Although the Church, the Body of Christ is the conduit through which God was channeling His blessing at that time, we know John was directed by the Spirit to confine his ministry to the *circumcision* (Israel) (Gal. 2:9).

Whether we believe the Book of Revelation was written at an early or later date is really a moot point if we understand the writing to be entirely futuristic. Those who may have reservations about John addressing future Israel should remember that the same is true of many Old Testament prophecies regarding the Tribulation. In fact, nearly half of the Book of Daniel falls into this very category. So then, the seven churches to whom John is writing are seven *future* Jewish assemblies located in Asia Minor (Rev. 1:11).

Theologians who reject the *futuristic view* have recognized some of the thorny issues associated with teaching that John was writing to seven churches in his day; consequently, they were compelled to spiritualize these churches, interpreting them to be seven stages of church history. But as Pastor J. C. O'Hair used to say, "Those who spiritualize the Scriptures tell spiritual lies." We are always to take a literal interpretation of the Word of God unless the context demands otherwise. Here, the evidence weighs heavily that these are *literal* Kingdom assemblies.

> "Blessed is he that readeth, and they that hear the words of this prophecy, and keep those things which are written therein: for the time is at hand" (Rev. 1:3).

A special blessing is reserved for those who not only read the words of this prophecy, but hear the prophetic vision preached, and more importantly, *obey* the message communicated to them. Seeing that there are a number of key prophecies which must be fulfilled at the very beginning of the Tribulation, it is impossible for any believer past or present to "keep those things" recorded in the Book of Revelation. One of these prophecies has to do with the ministry of the two witnesses, as we'll see in a moment!

When the apostle states, "The time is at hand," we must bear in mind that he is speaking to those who will be living when these events unfold.

> "John to the seven churches which are in Asia: Grace be unto you, and peace, from Him which is, and which was, and which is to come; and from the seven Spirits which are before His throne" (Rev. 1:4).

John would have naturally handed down the Book of Revelation to a small number of Kingdom believers that remained at the time, who then made sure it was included with the other manuscripts of the canon. They were well aware that God had set Israel aside in unbelief and had turned to the Gentiles; therefore, these saints understood the events recorded in the Apocalypse were entirely futuristic. This is confirmed by the text itself. John clearly states: "I was in the Spirit on the Lord's Day" (Rev. 1:10), that is, the coming *Day of the Lord*, which will begin with the seven-year Tribulation period.

Here again, the seven churches in Asia that John is addressing are *future* Kingdom assemblies that will be evangelized in the early part of the Tribulation. This is why he often writes in the present tense, for it's as if he were actually there as these events transpired during the course of the visions. Domitian may have banished John to Patmos as a punishment, but God used the occasion "for the Word of God, and for the testimony of Jesus Christ" (Rev. 1:9).

It should be remembered that, while Paul completed the Word of God in respect to its *extent* with the Mystery (I Cor. 13:10; Col. 1:25,26), John completed it in regard to its *depth* according to Prophecy (II Pet. 1:21; Rev. 1:3,9). Under the supervision of the Holy Spirit, John takes all the prophecies scattered throughout the prophetic Scriptures concerning "things to come," and places them in chronological order. He then fills in between the lines, as he was led by the Spirit, by giving connecting revelations so his readers might have a more detailed picture of future events *after* the Rapture of the Church.

GRACE AND PEACE
God the Father

> "John to the seven churches which are in Asia: Grace be unto you, and peace, from Him which is, and which was, and which is to come; and from the seven Spirits which are before His throne" (Rev. 1:4).

The number *seven* holds a prominent place in the Apocalypse. There are the seven churches in Asia, the seven Spirits, the seven stars, the seven seals, the seven trumpets, the seven thunders, the seven bowls, which contain the seven last plagues, etc. *Seven* in the Scriptures is the number of fullness, completeness; it speaks of spiritual perfection. When God finished creating the heavens and the earth in the beginning, He ended His work on the *seventh* day and rested (Gen. 2:2). His creation was complete and perfect!

But when Adam fell, paradise was lost due to sin. We give thanks that God has *promised* to redeem His creation from the bondage of corruption, the process of which is unfolded for us in the pages of *Revelation*. In the coming Day of the Lord, God will overthrow the kingdoms of this world and establish the Kingdom of His dear Son (Rev. 11:15). We are to understand, then, that the number *seven* is closely associated with the fullness of God's revelation and the fact that He always honors His Word.

The declaration of "grace and peace" in this passage is from God the Father in whom there is no variability or shadow of turning (James 1:17). He is "the high and lofty One that inhabited eternity" (Isa. 57:15). These Tribulation saints will be able to rest assured that "grace," God's freely given *influence* in their lives, will guide them through the dark days ahead. This is to be understood as "grace" within a dispensation, and should not be confused with the Dispensation of Grace. The eternal presence of the Father will be with them every step of the way; He will even give them the very words to speak when they are oppressed and made to stand before their enemies (Matt. 10:19,20). While the world will be in utter turmoil at the time, they will have an inner "peace" from God, Who is in control. Even in the face of martyrdom they will find peace in the fact that they will be with the Lord (Rev. 6:9-11).

The Seven Spirits

The declaration of grace and peace is also from the "seven Spirits which are before His throne." Some commentators believe this is a reference to the Holy Spirit and His sevenfold ministry, based on Isaiah 11:2. We do not believe this is the case because the seven spirits are said to be before the throne of God, which is a position of subordination and servitude. This certainly would not be true of the Spirit of God who is co-equal and co-eternal, for He is God!

These "seven spirits" who stand before the Lord are a *special class* of angelic beings who carry out the highest service of God. This was true in time past and will again be the case during the coming Day of the Lord. Gabriel, for example, is one of the seven spirits who stands before the throne.

> "And the angel answering said unto him [Zacharias], I am Gabriel, that stand in the presence of God; and am sent to speak unto thee, and to show thee these glad tidings" (Luke 1:19).

25

Michael, the archangel, is probably another one of the seven spirits who stands ready to carry out the just commands of God during the Tribulation.

> "And at that time shall Michael stand up, the great prince which standeth for the children of thy people: and there shall be a time of trouble, such as never was since there was a nation even to that same time: and at that time thy people shall be delivered" (Dan. 12:1).

It will be comforting to the Tribulation saints that these seven spirits are on their side, as their declaration of *grace* and *peace* demonstrates. They will be constantly ministering on behalf of these saints throughout the time known as Jacob's Trouble.

As we know, God created an innumerable host of angels in the beginning. In fact, we believe the creation of the angelic host was the first creative act of God. They actually *witnessed* the laying of the foundation of earth, "When the morning stars sang together, and all the sons of God shouted for joy" (Job 38:3-7). Angels are spirit beings who minister to those who are heirs of salvation. For example, during the Babylonian captivity, the angel Gabriel ministered more than once to the prophet Daniel (Dan. 9:20-23). He imparted to him the vision of the seventy weeks of years, the last week (7-year Tribulation) of which is under consideration here in our study of the Book of Revelation.

During the years of the captivity, Israel lived under the Gentile domination commonly known as the "times of the Gentiles" (Luke 21:24). Gabriel revealed to Daniel that the time was appointed when the creation would witness the *regathering* and *restoration* of Israel, at the close of the Tribulation when the everlasting Kingdom will be set up. When we turn to the Book of Revelation, we again witness how the ministry of angels will be very prominent as

Daniel's prophecy of the seventy weeks of years is literally fulfilled. They will be God's instruments of judgment as they pour out His undiluted wrath on this evil world. The writings of Daniel and Revelation have much in common in regard to God working through His angelic creation to implement the counsel of His will.

THE SON OF GOD

> "And from Jesus Christ, Who is the faithful witness, and the first begotten of the dead, and the Prince of the kings of the earth. Unto Him that loved us, and washed us from our sins in His own blood" (Rev. 1:5).

The declaration of "grace and peace" to those who endure the coming Tribulation is based upon what the Lord Jesus Christ accomplished on their behalf. He is the faithful witness! The word "witness" used in this passage by John is the Greek word *martus*, from which we get our English word *martyr*. When the Redeemer left Heaven's glory, He came to bear witness of the truth. Unlike those who suffer martyrdom for the sake of the truth however, no man took Christ's life from Him; rather, He had the power to lay down His life and the power to raise Himself from the dead (John 10:17,18).

With this in mind, He is "the first begotten of the dead." Christ trod the same path as all those before Him when He entered the valley of death—not for Himself, mind you, for death had no claim on Him because He was the sinless, spotless Lamb of God. Rather, He died for the *sins of His people*. The scope of redemption in prophecy is limited to Israel and those who would be saved through her. As the apostle says in this passage, "Unto Him that loved us, and washed us from our sins in His own blood." The pronoun *us* is speaking of the Apostle John and his countrymen who believed on the name of Christ, that He was the Anointed of Israel (John

27

20:31). They are the ones spoken of here that are "washed" or cleansed from their sins by His precious blood.

As the "firstborn of the dead," Christ conquered death and rose victoriously over it forevermore; therefore, He holds a unique position. While there were those who were miraculously brought back from the dead in time past, they all share one thing in common: They all died again and lie in the dust of the earth to this very hour. Christ, on the other hand, is the *first* from among the dead to receive a glorified, resurrected body. He alone has immortality (I Tim. 6:16). This will be particularly *consoling* to those who face martyrdom during the coming Tribulation, because to faithfully name the name of Christ will have grave consequences (Rev. 14:13). When they find themselves facing death, the hope of the resurrection will be the anchor of their souls. Of course, their hope is to be raised in the *first resurrection* at the Second Coming of Christ.

> "And hath made us kings and priests unto God and His Father; to Him be glory and dominion for ever and ever. Amen" (Rev. 1:6).

This language is completely foreign to the Church, the Body of Christ. If we are kings, as some suppose, who are our subjects? If we are the priests of God, what Gentile dare accept the office according to the Law without finding himself under the penalty of death? Where in the Old Testament or the New Testament are the Gentiles ever called priests or promised to be a kingdom of priests? We believe you will be hard-pressed to find such a passage, but we challenge you to search the Scriptures to see for yourself.

You see, the priesthood was specifically given to the chosen nation of Israel under the law. Only those of the tribe of Levi were permitted to minister in the priest's office. Those who entered this office did so through a water ceremony, which symbolized the cleansing of their sins (Ex. 29:4). The Aaronic priesthood, which would give way to the superior order of Melchizedec (Christ), foreshadowed the day when the entire nation would become a kingdom of priests. Three passages bear witness to this truth.

The Law: "And ye shall be unto me a kingdom of priests, and an holy nation" (Ex. 19:6).

The Prophets: "But ye shall be named the Priests of the LORD: men shall call you the Ministers of our God" (Isa. 61:6).

The Kingdom Gospel: "But ye are a chosen generation, a royal priesthood, an holy nation, a peculiar people" (I Pet. 2:9).

Israel's induction into the priesthood began with John the Baptist who baptized believing Israelites with water. So then, having been cleansed from their sins by the blood of Christ, the Apostle John confirms in Revelation 1:6 that believing Israelites will be *made* the priests of God in the coming Kingdom. They will minister in the holy things of God, not merely they of the tribe of Levi, but *all* the tribes of the chosen nation. This will be in fulfillment of the promise.

They will also be *made* "kings" and their subjects will be the Gentiles. "Thus saith the LORD of hosts; In those days it shall come to pass, that ten men shall take hold out of all languages of the nations, even shall take hold of the skirt of him that is a Jew, saying, We will go with you: for we have heard that God is with you" (Zech. 8:23).

WHICH COMING?

"Behold, He cometh with clouds; and every eye shall see Him, and they also which pierced Him: and all kindreds of the earth shall wail because of Him. Even so, Amen" (Rev. 1:7).

Although many ignore the fact that there are two distinct returns of Christ taught in the Scriptures, God does not ignore it. Here again, whatsoever God has separated let no man join together; to do so is to confuse the two programs of God. As we will see throughout this study, the Book of Revelation is perfectly aligned, by the Spirit of God, with Old Testament prophecy and the Kingdom gospel. If this is always kept in mind, we will find that the prophetic Scriptures actually interpret most of the symbolism found in the Apocalypse.

There is absolutely no question that John is speaking about the Second Coming of Christ in verse 7. Like most authors, John is writing the introduction to the book (Chapter 1) *after* he saw all the events of the Apocalypse unfold. The actual revelation of Christ's return to earth isn't revealed until Chapter 19. By placing it in the introduction, John wanted his readers to understand that the troublous times ahead would abruptly end when Christ returns in a flaming fire of vengeance to execute judgment upon their enemies. He will have the final word in the affairs of men. "For it is written, Vengeance is mine; I will repay, saith the Lord" (Rom. 12:19).

Unrelated to the Rapture, which is the *invisible* return of Christ for the Church, His Second Coming will be *visible*: "every eye shall see Him." Then John is careful to point out "and they also which pierced Him." This is a clear reference to apostate Israel; they were the ones who cried, "Crucify Him, crucify Him," and "Away with Him, away with Him, crucify Him," to which Pilate responded, "Shall I crucify your King?" Amazingly, the chief priests answered, "We have no king but Caesar" (John 19:15).

Peter rolls out the rhetorical artillery after the crucifixion of Christ and charges his countrymen with the death of their own Messiah. He paints such a vivid picture that it was as if the blood of guilt was dripping off the ends of their fingers. Peter plainly states, "Ye have taken, and by wicked hands have crucified and slain" (Acts 2:23). In his second Pentecostal address he made it clear they had "killed the Prince of life." But, we rejoice greatly that God raised Him from the dead and He's coming again to execute judgment on those who pierced Him. But are not those who were responsible for committing the evil deed, dead? Indeed, dead as a doornail! A comparison of two passages will help shed some light on the dilemma:

Christ's first coming (and crucifixion): "Then answered all the people, and said, His blood be on us, *and on our children*" (Matt. 27:25).

Christ's Second Coming: "And they shall look upon Me whom they have pierced, and they shall mourn for Him, as one mourneth for his only son, and shall be in bitterness for Him, as one that is in bitterness for his firstborn. In that day shall there be a great mourning in Jerusalem" (Zech. 12:10,11).

You see, in the coming Tribulation, Israel, as a people, will *still* be in denial that Jesus was their Messiah and that they were responsible for His crucifixion (Acts 5:28). But when they look up and see Him coming in power and great glory they will not be able to deny their senses. They will mourn because of Him.

"And all kindreds of the earth shall wail because of Him." This refers to those who blasphemed Him and received the mark of the beast. Unlike the Rapture, when the Lord will return to the first heaven, at the Second Coming the soles of His feet will stand on the Mount of Olives (Zech. 14:4). He will then enter the valley of Megiddo where the blood of the armies of the earth will flow as high as the horses' bridles at the battle of Armageddon (Rev. 14:20). Their cry will be great when they see Him coming. Men's hearts will fail within them.

The practical lesson here is this: The clock is ticking as these events draw closer; time is short as the days grow darker. May God give us a greater burden for those who are unknowingly walking on the rotten planks over Hell, not realizing the terrible end that awaits them. It is our desire that the words of this commentary will challenge each of us to have a greater appreciation that we've been spared the fierceness of His anger, for "It is a fearful thing to fall into the hands of the living God" (Heb. 10:31). When was the last time you thanked God that you are living in the Age of Grace? Do it today. The Lord is waiting to hear from you!

A JOURNEY THROUGH TIME

"I am Alpha and Omega, the Beginning and the Ending, saith the Lord, Which is, and Which was, and Which is to come, the Almighty" (Rev. 1:8).

In the Book of Revelation, Christ is the *Alpha* and the *Omega*. *Alpha* and *omega* are the first and last letters of the Greek alphabet. The Lord knows the end from the beginning because He has planned and purposed all things according to the counsel of His will. In essence, this is the very foundation of prophecy. As an eminent Bible teacher has said: "What is prophecy, but history written in advance?"

Ottman states concerning the expression, "Who [which] is, and who [which] was, and who [which] is to come," that it "defines for us, in a limited way of course, the meaning of the name Jehovah. At the burning bush, Moses asked for His name, and the answer was, 'I AM THAT I AM' (Ex. 3:14). This is what the name Jehovah means. He is the

Self-Existent One, unchangeably such, the same yesterday, and to-day, and forever. As He is, so has He ever been, and so shall He ever be throughout all the ages of ages. Let man be what he will; with Jehovah there is no change."[1] Of course, Brother Ottman is speaking about the *unchanging character* of God, but we must never lose sight of the fact that the Scriptures undeniably teach that He does indeed change His dealings with mankind from time to time.

Although time travel is impossible for man, nothing is impossible with God. He is eternal, all-knowing, all-powerful, and ever-present. Just as Enoch, Elijah, and Phillip were transported to another place in a moment of time, the Apostle John was carried away in the Spirit to the future Day of the Lord (Heb. 11:5; II Kings 2:11,12; Acts 8:39,40 cf. Rev. 1:9,10). (And you thought your vacation last summer was the trip of a lifetime!) Does all this sound farfetched? Not to the believer who views it through the eye of faith! What saith the Scriptures?

> "I John, who also am your brother, and companion in [the] Tribulation, and in the Kingdom and patience of Jesus Christ, was in the isle that is called Patmos, for the Word of God, and for the testimony of Jesus Christ. I was in the Spirit on the Lord's day, and heard behind me a great voice, as of a trumpet" (Rev. 1:9,10).

This is John, the beloved, who laid his head on the breast of Jesus at the Last Supper. He was one of the twelve apostles of the Kingdom, and as far as we know, he was the last surviving member of the group when he penned these words. According to John, he had been banished to the isle of Patmos by the Roman Emperor Domitian.[2] The banishment was meant to be a death sentence for the aged apostle, but God turned the ill intent into an unforgettable revelation of His dear Son.

As a Hebrew addressing Hebrews, John identifies himself with his kinsmen after the flesh. He is their brother and companion in troublous times. If we consult the original language here, we learn that the definite article precedes the noun, *Tribulation*. Consequently, John is their companion during "the" seven-year Tribulation and the Millennium that follows. These are the things "which must shortly come to pass," spoken of in verse 1, and so naturally, John is writing to those who will be living at that day. This is confirmed for us by the apostle's next statement: "I was in the Spirit on the Lord's Day."

Tradition teaches that the Lord's Day is Sunday, the day Christians customarily worship, but this is foreign to the Scriptures. The Lord's Day or *Day of the Lord* is a clear reference to an extended period of time that covers seven years of Tribulation, the Second Coming of Christ, the binding of Satan in the bottomless pit, the judgment of Israel and the nations, the Millennial reign of Christ, the battle of Gog and Magog, the Great White Throne Judgment, and the purging of the heavens and earth by fire.

In the Old Testament, the Hebrew phrase, *Day of the Lord*, can only be translated, "Day of the Lord," without exception. However, in the Greek of the New Testament, it can be translated "the Lord's Day" or "Day of the Lord." Either way it is translated, it is referring to the same period of time. As John was transported to this future day, he was seated in the balcony, as it were, and recorded all the events that unfolded before his very eyes.

> "What thou seest, write in a book, and send it unto the seven churches which are in Asia; unto Ephesus, and unto Smyrna, and unto Pergamos, and unto Thyatira, and unto Sardis, and unto Philadelphia, and unto Laodicea. And I turned to see the voice that

spake with me. And being turned, I saw seven golden candlesticks" (Rev. 1:11,12).

Having learned that John was writing to his kinsmen in the coming Day of the Lord, we read that he is instructed to record what he saw and send it to seven Jewish assemblies. This was accomplished when the Book of Revelation was included in the canon of Holy Scripture. The same can be said of all the Old Testament prophecies regarding this period (e.g., Ezek. 37:1-28).

When the trump sounds and we are caught up to be with the Lord at the Rapture, all believers will have been removed from the earth. This logically raises the following question: How will those who make up these seven churches in Asia be evangelized and formed at the beginning of the Tribulation? Before we address this question, we must first consider whether or not there will be a gap between the Rapture of the Church and the beginning of the Tribulation.

Many capable Bible teachers believe that it will be needful for God to place an intervening period of one year between these two events before He resumes His prophetic program. They feel it will take at least this amount of time for the Temple to be rebuilt so as to insure that the Antichrist can establish a covenant with Israel based upon the sacrificial system. Others believe that after the Rapture takes place the prophetic program will be reintroduced for one generation (40 years) before Daniel's Seventieth Week (7-year Tribulation) begins. These positions are well worth your thoughtful consideration.

With that said, however, the Scriptures make no mention of a gap between the Mystery program and the continuation of prophecy. Since we are living in God's parenthetical Age of Grace, which was *hidden* from ages and generations past, Paul would have naturally been the one to reveal if there was to be a brief interval before the Day of the Lord. But the apostle is silent on the matter! In fact, Paul seems to indicate that the Antichrist will begin his reign of terror *immediately* following the departure of the Church (II Thes. 2:3,7,8) We believe when the trump sounds at the Rapture, it will break the silence of the present dispensation as God declares war on this Christ-rejecting world. This will mark the beginning of the Tribulation. These two events will be simultaneous.

But there is even a more important issue that is often overlooked in this dialog. If there is an interval after the Rapture, God will be leaving Himself without a human testimony and redemptive program upon the earth, which is something He has never done in the past. We believe the stage will have already been set behind the scenes for the immediate fulfillment of prophecy following the catching away of the Church (e.g., II Thes. 2:7,8). It is true that the sacrificial system will have to be in place at the beginning of the Tribulation, but until the Temple is built, this could easily be accomplished by temporarily using the Tabernacle, as they did in the days of King Solomon. Of course, some believe that Israel will rebuild the Temple in her own strength near the end of the current age, and that may well be the case. It would then simply be used by God to accomplish His purpose in the coming Day of the Lord.

THE TWO WITNESSES

"And I will give power unto my two witnesses, and they shall prophesy a thousand two hundred and three-score days [3½ years], clothed in sackcloth" (Rev. 11:3).

We believe that those who make up the seven churches in Asia will be the fruits of the two witnesses and the 144,000 (which we'll cover in more detail later). While it is generally believed that they conduct their ministry during the last half of the Tribulation, this view does not align itself with the Scriptures. We know, for instance, that God pronounces *three woes* in the Book of Revelation. The first woe is fulfilled in the first part of the Tribulation (Rev. 9:12), the second woe in the mid-part (Rev. 11:14), and the third during the last part (Rev. 12:12). This obviously indicates that the two witnesses will suffer martyrdom in the middle of the Tribulation, since the second woe is a direct consequence of their deaths (Rev. 11:7-14).

As the sound of the trump that accompanies the Rapture fades in the distance, the two witnesses will immediately appear in Jerusalem, where they will prophesy for 3½ years in accordance with the Great Commission (Acts 1:8 cf. Rev. 11:8). With the prophetic program reinstated, signs, miracles, and wonders will accompany their proclamation of the Kingdom gospel.

These two servants of the Lord are called olive trees that *stand* before God (Rev. 11:4). The symbolic usage of the olive tree in the Scriptures is to identify God's witnesses (Rom. 11:16-24). With the cutting off of the Gentiles at the Rapture, Israel will again be grafted back into her rightful position as the witnesses of God, which the two witnesses here in Revelation represent. They will faithfully bear testimony that Jesus is the Christ (Messiah), the very Son of God (John 20:31).

On the day of Pentecost, when Peter preached the Kingdom gospel in connection with the Spirit's miraculous manifestations, it produced amazing results: Three thousand were saved in *one day*. A few days later, an additional two thousand souls were added. As dawn breaks on the Tribulation, God is going to *resume* the prophetic program at the point when it was interrupted, shortly after Pentecost.

Subsequently, the testimony and prophecies of these two witnesses will produce the same results as the ministry of the twelve at Pentecost. In fact, they will be responsible for the conversion of the 144,000 who are said to be the *first fruits* redeemed unto God (Rev. 14:1-5). These are 144,000 Jewish missionaries who will evangelize the lost to Christ, which helps us to understand how the seven churches in Asia will come into existence. We will identify these two witnesses in an upcoming chapter, but suffice it to say for now that they are sent from the Lord at the very beginning of the Tribulation so that the testimony of God on earth is *uninterrupted*. If any man attempts to harm them in the days of their prophecy, he will experience the swift judgment of God (Rev. 11:5).

With the stage now set, the first vision that the Apostle John received is a vision of what takes place on the earth. What we are about to learn in the next chapter can only be described as indescribable!

2

The Judge of All the Earth

"And I turned to see the voice that spake with me.
And being turned, I saw seven golden candlesticks;
And in the midst of the seven candlesticks one like
unto the Son of Man."

—Revelation 1:12,13a

THE SEVEN GOLDEN CANDLESTICKS
AND THE SON OF MAN

The initial vision that John received of the Son of Man is
the first of many that will require total reliance on the Word
of God, to enable us to interpret the wealth of symbolic language. As the Apostle John turned to see who was speaking to him in the vision, he saw the Judge of all the earth
standing in the midst of seven golden candlesticks. We give
thanks that we are not left to our own human reasoning as
to what these seven golden candlesticks represent; the Lord
Himself tells us in verse 20.

"The mystery of the seven stars which thou sawest
in my right hand, and the seven golden candlesticks.
The seven stars are the angels of the seven churches:
and the seven candlesticks which thou sawest are the
seven churches" (Rev. 1:20).

This passage should help to ease our minds that interpreting of the signs and symbols in the Book of Revelation
isn't as intimidating as we first may have thought. The
seven golden candlesticks, then, are seven churches that
will be located in Asia Minor in the future Day of the Lord.

They are identified in Revelation 1:11 as Ephesus, Smyrna, Pergamos, Thyatira, Sardis, Philadelphia, and Laodicea. Just as local assemblies today are comprised of believers who make up the true Church, the Body of Christ, these seven Jewish assemblies in similar fashion are an integral part of the Kingdom Church. Therefore, the special revelation that the Lord is about to deliver to these seven assemblies is meant to be distributed among all Kingdom believers.

The Greek word *luchnia* (candlestick) derives its meaning from the Greek term *luchnos* (lampstand). Both words are closely associated with illumination. When we consider the seven golden lampstands, our minds naturally return to the golden lampstand in the Old Testament Tabernacle (Ex. 25:31-40). Although there are similarities between the two, they serve a different purpose. The lampstand in the Tabernacle was *one* stand with seven lamps that were attached to each of the branches. It provided light for the sanctuary in the holy place where no natural light was permitted. This lampstand foreshadowed Christ who is the light of the world. He is the light! (John 8:12).

Here in the Book of Revelation we are introduced to seven *individual* lampstands, each of which is to exhibit the light of Christ. You see, these Jewish assemblies will be responsible to shine individually as lights in the midst of the darkness of the Antichrist Kingdom. They are to be a light to the lost sheep of the house of Israel, pointing them to the Good Shepherd of the sheep and the green pastures of the coming Kingdom. In so doing, they will glorify their heavenly Father through their good works, as the Lord stated during His earthly ministry:

> "Ye are the light of the world. A city that is set on an hill cannot be hid. Neither do men light a candle, and put it under a bushel, but on a candlestick [lampstand];

and it giveth light unto all that are in the house. Let your light so shine before men, that they may see your good works, and glorify your Father which is in heaven" (Matt. 5:14-16).

The Son of Man

"And in the midst of the seven candlesticks one like unto the Son of Man" (Rev. 1:13a).

The title *Son of Man* has a twofold purpose in its usage. First, it is closely associated with the humanity of Christ, that He came in the flesh. As the designation suggests, He is identified as a member of the human race. Second, the title is used to designate His sovereignty, that He is the Judge of all the earth.

According to our passage, the Apostle John saw "one like unto the Son of Man" standing in the center of the seven churches. At first glance, it may appear strange that John seemed so uncertain as to whether or not the One whom he saw was the Lord Jesus. But we must bear in mind that he had never seen the Lord as He is depicted here in the Apocalypse. This gives new meaning to the concept of an eye-opening experience! Prior to this vision, John had only been acquainted with the Son of Man in his humanity. He knew Him as the *lowly* Jesus who was merciful and compassionate to all those who came to Him. He observed as the Lord suffered beyond comprehension at the hands of evil man. John remembered well "when He was reviled, reviled not again; when He suffered, He threatened not; but committed Himself to Him that judgeth righteously" (I Pet. 2:23).

But now the scene has changed dramatically. Christ is revealed here as a Judge whose appearance is so fearsome that it took the apostle by surprise. Because Christ is God manifested in the flesh, He is the perfect Judge, having the scales of justice balanced between being a Member of the Godhead and a Member of humanity. For this reason, God the Father has entrusted all future judgment to His dear Son (John 5:22,26,27). None who deserve justice will escape justice! It is obvious from the scene before us that the Judge of all the earth is prepared to return to the earth in a flaming fire of vengeance to execute judgment upon all evildoers.

The title *Son of Man* is never used by the Apostle Paul in his Gentile epistles, and for good reason: We no longer know Christ after the flesh, nor will we witness His Second Coming to judge mankind. We know Christ today as the glorified Lord of Heaven, lavishing the members of His Body with the riches of His grace. We know Him as the Savior who died for the sins of the world, but the time is fast approaching when God will speak to the world in His wrath. Those who continue in their rejection of the Savior will one day face Him as their Judge, as the following story illustrates:

"Some years ago a man driving down the streets of one of our great cities lost control of his horses and was in danger of being dashed to death. Suddenly, there sprang out into the street a man who, seizing the horses by the bit, stopped them in their mad career and saved the driver's life.

"By a singular coincidence, years afterwards the man whose life was saved was on trial before the one who had stopped the horses, who sat in the judge's chair. The trial was ended; the lawyers had made the plea and the jury had returned with its verdict, when the judge said, 'Have you anything to say why sentence should not be pronounced upon you?' Then, rising, trembling with great emotion, he said: 'Judge, don't you remember me?' And the judge said once again, 'Have you anything to say why sentence should not be pronounced?' And then he said, 'Why, Judge, I am the man you saved; have mercy, have mercy.' And with a look full of pity, his honor replied, 'I do remember you and I am very sorry for you, but then I was your savior, and today I am your judge;' and the sentence of death was passed.

"Today our Savior stands waiting to be merciful, with tears in His eyes....But one day the picture will change, and He will be our judge to say, 'Depart, for I never knew you.' God save us from that day."[1]

Interestingly, the prophetic Scriptures depict the Lord *sitting* at the right hand of the Father until all His enemies are made His footstool (Psa. 110:1). In short, these enemies are those who deny He is Messiah and have oppressed His people. Since the days when Israel was in bondage to the Egyptians until the present, one attempt after another has been made to eradicate her from the face of the earth, like an unwanted plague among the nations. The Antichrist would nearly accomplish this very thing, if it were not for the Lord's intervention. The chosen nation looks forward with great anticipation to the fulfillment of the psalmists' words:

"Arise, O LORD, in thine anger, lift up thyself because of the rage of mine enemies: and awake for me to the judgment that thou hast commanded" (Psa. 7:6).

"Arise, O LORD; let not man prevail: let the heathen be judged in thy sight" (Psa. 9:19).

"Arise, O God, judge the earth: for thou shalt inherit all nations" (Psa. 82:8).

In the panoramic view that is set before us by John, the Son of Man is *standing* in the midst of the seven churches, clothed in a long, flowing garment down to the foot. Throughout the Apocalypse, the Son of Man is always said to be standing (Rev. 3:20; 5:6; 14:1; etc.). The Apostle John is describing for us the dawn of the Tribulation period known as Jacob's Trouble. While the heavens are silent today, God is soon going to speak to the world in His indignation for its blatant denial of who He is. He will address, in no uncertain terms, the outright rejection of His Word and the unmitigated rebellion against what He accomplished for mankind at Calvary. Men will believe the lie of evolution before they will acknowledge God to be the Creator and the Sustainer of all things. Medical science will tirelessly search the invisible things of creation to extend life, but openly reject Christ who freely gives life and life eternal to all who believe. Hear me and hear me well, the day is soon coming when God will address their unbelief and unrelenting persecution of His people.

"For the great day of His wrath is come; and who shall be able to stand?" (Rev. 6:17). The answer to the question is only found in the Scriptures! The Judge stands prepared, according to John's vision, to pour out the fierceness of His anger against sin. This will commence immediately after He gives instructions to the seven churches in Asia.

Here's an example of what lies ahead: Midway through the Tribulation, a swarm of locusts/demonic beings will be unleashed from the bottomless pit and torment men for five months. Recently on a Southwest Airlines flight from Phoenix, Arizona, a scorpion fell from an overhead bin and stung a passenger on the leg. It goes without saying that he was in excruciating pain for days with a swollen leg. These infernal beings that ascend out of the pit will afflict men with a scorpion-like sting, the pain of which doesn't last merely for days, but months. Men will seek death, but it will flee from them under this judgment (Rev. 9:1-6).

If you know the Lord as your personal Savior, before you retire this evening, don't forget to thank Him for delivering you, as a member of the Body of Christ, from the wrath to come!

PREPARATION FOR BATTLE

"And in the midst of the seven candlesticks one like
unto the Son of Man, clothed with a garment down to
the foot, and girt about the paps with a golden girdle.
His head and His hairs were white like wool, as white
as snow; and His eyes were as a flame of fire; And His
feet like unto fine brass, as if they burned in a furnace;
and His voice as the sound of many waters. And He
had in His right hand seven stars: and out of His mouth
went a sharp two-edged sword: and His countenance
was as the sun shineth in His strength. And when I
saw Him, I fell at His feet as dead" (Rev. 1:13-17a).

In time past, all those who were given the privilege of
stepping into the veiled glory of Christ's presence immediately fell at the feet of His eternal majesty. This was true
of Moses, Aaron, Joshua, Isaiah, and Paul. John was so
overwhelmed by the appearance of the Son of Man that
he, too, fell at His feet as dead, but for a somewhat different reason. As we have established, he was accustomed
to seeing the Son of Man in His humiliation; this was the
first time he had ever seen Him as the Judge of the earth.
If we contrast Christ's humiliation with His appearance
as Judge in the Apocalypse, it will help us to understand
John's astonishment better. With sincere appreciation, we
take the liberty here to present Leon Tucker's observation
of these two periods in our Lord's life:

"*In Christ's humiliation,* He was the lowly Savior who
was despised and rejected of men; *here,* in the Book of Revelation He is the sovereign Judge of the universe. *In the
days of His humiliation,* He hung on a cruel tree amidst
two thieves; *here,* He is standing in the midst of seven gold-
en lampstands in supreme glory. *Then,* He was unclothed
and displayed in nakedness while the soldiers parted His
garments among themselves; *here,* He is robed in a garment

of a High Priest and Judge. *Then,* He girded Himself with a towel to wash the disciples' feet in all humility; *here,* He is gird about with a golden girdle, which speaks of deity. He is prepared for battle! *Then,* His head was encircled with a crown of thorns; *here,* He is the Ancient of days whose head and hair is white as snow.

"*In Christ's humiliation,* He wept over Jerusalem; *here,* His eyes are as a flame of fire exposing the ways of the evil one. *In the days of His humiliation,* His feet were pierced through with a large spike; *here,* His feet are as fine brass burnished in a furnace, which speaks of His enemies who are about to be judged and crushed under His feet. *In the days of His flesh,* He offered up prayers and supplications in meekness: *in John's vision,* His voice is like the sound of a mighty waterfall—powerful and full of majesty! *Then,* they nailed His right hand to the Cross; *here,* in His sovereign good pleasure He holds the believer in His right hand. *Then,* out of His mouth came the words of life; *here,* a sword to smite the nations and rule with a rod of iron. *Instead* of a 'visage marred more than any man,' His countenance *in John's vision* is 'as the sun shineth in his strength.'"[2]

> "And in the midst of the seven candlesticks one like unto the Son of Man, clothed with a garment down to the foot" (v. 13).

We want to add to Brother Tucker's insightful comments that the garment in which the Son of Man appeared is the same type of regal garment that was worn by the High Priest and the Judges in Old Testament times (Lev. 16:4). The Lord will effectively execute both of these roles in the coming Tribulation and Kingdom. As He stands in the midst of the seven churches, He is the High Priest of those who place their faith in Him. He lives to make intercession for His own. These Kingdom believers will find comfort and strength in this when they face one fiery trial after another at the hands of the Antichrist. They will be able to say with all confidence, "For we have not an high priest which cannot be touched with the feeling of our infirmities; but was in all points tempted [tested] like as we are, yet without sin" (Heb. 4:15).

Within these assemblies, however, the enemy will sow tares to corrupt the truth of God. These deceivers will say they are Jews, but in reality they belong to the synagogue of Satan (Rev. 2:9). The Age of Grace will have passed; consequently, when the Judge returns He will tread the winepress alone, and trample in His fury those who follow the Beast, and their blood will stain His *garments*, for the day of vengeance is in His heart (Isa. 63:2-4).

Around the Son of Man's torso was a golden girdle, or what we would call a belt (v. 13). Gold is a symbol of deity, and justifiably so here, because the Son of Man is also the Son of God. The girdle here speaks of strength. In biblical times, a man would gather up his long, flowing garment, securing it around his waist with a belt in preparation for battle. John also noted that "His head and His hairs were white like wool, as white as snow" (v. 14), which speaks of purity, white being a symbol of righteousness in the Scriptures (Rev. 19:8). Unlike the world where there are often miscarriages of justice due to corruption, God's judgment is always just. Thus "His eyes were as a flame of fire," searching and exposing the evil deeds of men.

The apostle adds, "And His feet [were] like unto fine brass, as if they burned in a furnace" (v. 15). Since the brazen altar represented judgment in the Old Testament, we can confidently conclude the same is true here, the reference to *fine brass* being the execution of it with precision. In other words, the Son of Man will overthrow His adversaries with the precision of a laser beam. Finally, John says, "His voice

[was] as the sound of many waters." When the Son of Man spoke, He did so with such authority and power that it will literally cause the earth to quake in the coming Day of the Lord (Rev. 16:17-19).

FEAR NOT!

"And He laid His right hand upon me, saying unto me, Fear not; I am the first and the last: I am He that liveth, and was dead; and, behold, I am alive for evermore, Amen; and have the keys of hell and of death" (Rev. 1:17b,18).

The voice of the sound of many waters that will strike terror into the heart of the unsaved in the future Tribulation will be music to the ears of the believer. John was so overcome by the vision of the Son of Man that he collapsed at His feet in humble adoration. Our Lord compassionately lays His right hand on the apostle affectionately known as the disciple whom Jesus loved, and says, *"Fear not!"* If there was any doubt in John's mind as to Who was standing before him, it vanished like the morning mist when he heard those familiar words. John undoubtedly recalled the first time he heard them. It was the day the Lord miraculously filled the net of the disciples with fish, after they had fished all night and caught nothing. **"Fear not**; from henceforth thou shalt catch men" (Luke 5:10). They all dropped their nets and followed Him.

After saying, "Fear not," the Lord adds, "I am the first and the last." The terminology in verse 8, "I am Alpha and Omega, the beginning and the ending," and here in verse 17, "I am the first and the last," speaks to the fact that Christ is the great I AM. He is the eternal God! This is why Isaiah states, in Isaiah 9:6, that a "child is born" (Christ's birth at Bethlehem), but a "Son is given," which validates that Christ is the eternal Son of God.

The Lord's next statement, "I am He that liveth, and was dead; and, behold, I am alive for evermore," is to be understood in the context of His incarnation when the Word was made flesh. With this in mind, the threefold ministry of Christ is divided as follows: "He that liveth" covers the period of thirty-three years that He dwelt among us as a Jew under the Law; "and was dead," speaks of His death at Calvary; "and, behold, I am alive for evermore," refers to His bodily resurrection from the dead. As a result, He has the "keys of hell [Greek *Hades*] and of death." The power that Satan once held over *Hades* and death was lost when Christ conquered death and victoriously rose over it (Col. 2:14,15).

If you possess the keys to a safety deposit box, then you have the right to access it. This is also true of Christ. Because of His finished work, He has the *authority* over the unseen realm of the dead and death itself. As it has been said, "No man can die apart from divine permission even though afflicted by Satan and in trial and trouble."[3] The fact that Christ rose from the dead guarantees the believer's future resurrection from the dead. This is the hope of Israel! (Acts 23:6 cf. 28:20).

When the Lord gave Peter the keys of the Kingdom, He essentially gave the apostle the *authority* to act on His behalf regarding matters of the Kingdom. This, however, did not include the power over death and Hades, which belongs to Christ alone. Even though the Tribulation saints will be marked for death by the Antichrist, they need not fear death, for Christ has power over it. He is the resurrection and the life! This will be especially consoling during the time of Jacob's Trouble, seeing as how saints will be martyred in unprecedented numbers. History bears out that the Holocaust of World War II was primarily confined to

Europe, but the one that lies ahead will be *global* in its scope (Rev. 6:7-11). The cost of testifying of Christ in that day will be extremely high.

THE APOSTLE'S COMMISSION TO WRITE

"Write the things which thou hast seen, and the things which are, and the things which shall be hereafter" (Rev. 1:19).

The traditional interpretation of this passage goes something like this: "Write the things which thou hast seen" is the past, limited to the vision of the Son of Man found in Chapter 1. "And the things which are," the present, refers to Chapters 2 and 3, where we are presented with the seven historical stages of the Church, the Body of Christ. "And the things which shall be hereafter" speaks of the future, things to come beginning in Chapter 4.

This particular interpretation leaves much to be desired for several reasons. First and foremost, we have already established from the Scriptures that the entirety of the Book of Revelation, from Chapter 1 to Chapter 22, is futuristic. This explains why the Apostle John never makes any reference to the Church, the Body of Christ.

A better explanation is that John was to give a "record of the Word of God, and of the testimony of Jesus Christ, **and of all things that he saw**" (Rev. 1:2). In other words, when the Lord states, "Write the things which thou hast seen," John was to record *all* the visions he had received, from beginning to end, which would have included the vision of the Son of Man in Chapter 1. For example, "And I **saw**, and behold a white horse: and He that sat on him had a bow" (Rev. 6:2a). "And I **saw** another angel fly in the midst of heaven, having the everlasting gospel to preach unto them that dwell on the earth" (Rev. 14:6a).

Chapter 1 actually serves as an *Introduction* to the Apocalypse, as we noted earlier. Most authors, myself included, normally write the *Introduction* to a book after the rest of it is finished. This way, the author is familiar with the entire content of the writing for which the *Introduction* is a brief summation. If you read Chapter 1 of Revelation thoughtfully, it is evident that John is summarizing what he wrote about in other parts of the book. This is especially true of the first eleven verses.

Next, the apostle was to record "the things that **are**." Many believe the Apocalypse is a closed book and therefore can never be understood; however, they fail to understand that, in many cases, the book interprets itself. The "things that **are**" simply means that John was to explain various aspects of the symbolism of the Apocalypse—that is, what they actually *signify*. For example, if we wonder what the seven stars signify in the right hand of the Son of Man, John tells us, "The seven stars **are** the angels [messengers] of the seven churches" (Rev. 1:16 cf. 1:20). If we ponder the meaning of the "mystery of the woman, and of the beast that carrieth her, which hath the seven heads and ten horns," in Revelation 17, once again, the apostle interprets it for us. "The seven heads **are** seven mountains," or kingdoms, which have seven kings. "And the ten horns which thou sawest **are** ten kings," none of whom have a kingdom (Rev. 17:7 cf. 17:9,10,12).

Finally, John was to record, "the things which shall be **hereafter**." One thing we know about the Old Testament is that it doesn't give us a chronological order of things to come. John, on the other hand, gives us a sequence of events from beginning to end, which sometimes includes parenthetical segments. He records for us the things that will *come to pass*, for instance, "Come up hither, and I will show thee things which must be **hereafter**" (Rev. 4:1).

"**And after these things** I saw four angels standing on the four corners of the earth, holding the four winds of the earth, that the wind should not blow on the earth, nor on the sea, nor on any tree" (Rev. 7:1). "**And after these things** I saw another angel come down from heaven, having great power" (Rev. 18:1).[3]

> "The mystery of the seven stars which thou sawest in my right hand, and the seven golden candlesticks. The seven stars are the angels of the seven churches: and the seven candlesticks which thou sawest are the seven churches" (Rev. 1:20).

The description of the Son of Man woven throughout the narrative leaves little doubt that judgment awaits this sin-cursed world. But we rejoice on behalf of these Kingdom believers that they will be *secure*, even if they suffer martyrdom at the hands of the Antichrist. This is substantiated by John's statement, "He had in His right hand seven stars" (v. 16). As we will see, these seven stars are the messengers or pastors of the seven assemblies. Even though the Kingdom saints in time past never enjoyed the assurance of their salvation as we do today, they were nevertheless eternally secure (John 10:27-29). This will be true of the future Kingdom saints as well. The seven messengers being held in the right hand of the Son of Man are representative of this very truth.

A WORD TO THE WISE IS SUFFICIENT

A railroad crossing can be a dangerous place, especially when a motorist thinks he can disregard the warning signals with impunity. A few years ago, a 76-year-old woman from southern California thought she could beat an oncoming commuter train by crossing the tracks, with tragic results. Witnesses said she ignored the flashing red lights and swerved around the gates that had just descended into their horizontal position. The train hit the side of the woman's car at a high rate of speed, killing her instantly.

The distance and speed of a train approaching an intersection are extremely difficult to judge because the engine and the car crossing the tracks are traveling perpendicular to one another. The train is actually closer than it appears. Depending on the speed of the train, there's approximately 15 seconds from the time the gates are down to when the train enters the intersection.

I've spoken to a number of engineers over the years who have shared with me that people just don't understand the danger they place themselves and their families in when they try to beat a train: "People seem to think we can stop on a dime, which is certainly not the case." An eight-car commuter train traveling 79 mph takes approximately 5,280 feet or 1 mile to stop. A 150-car freight train traveling 30 mph takes 3,500 feet or 2/3 of a mile to stop.

Failing to heed the warning lights at a railroad crossing can have calamitous results. The same is true regarding the spiritual things of God. If the watchmen of the Lord's people, in this case the pastors of the seven churches, fail to adequately warn them of danger, will the Lord hold them blameless? On the other hand, if the Kingdom saints are warned but fail to heed the warnings of God, do not they bear the responsibility at the coming judgment? The Apostle John took his role as a watchman very seriously. He was faithful to record all the events of the Apocalypse, thereby *warning* the pastors of the seven churches in Asia not to take these things lightly. But what will be their response to these solemn warnings of God? The next three chapters will answer this question for us!

3

The Kingdom Church at Ephesus and Smyrna

"What thou seest, write in a book, and send it unto the seven churches which are in Asia; unto Ephesus, and unto Smyrna, and unto Pergamos, and unto Thyatira, and unto Sardis, and unto Philadelphia, and unto Laodicea."

—*Revelation 1:11*

THE JEWISH ASSEMBLY AT EPHESUS

The story is told "of pioneers who were making their way across one of the central states to a distant place that had been opened up for homesteading. They traveled in covered wagons drawn by oxen, and progress was necessarily slow. One day they were horrified to note a long line of smoke in the west, stretching for miles across the prairie, and soon it was evident that the dried grass was burning fiercely and coming toward them rapidly. They had crossed a river the day before but it would be impossible to go back to that before the flames would be upon them. "One man only seemed to have understanding as to what could be done. He gave the command to set fire to the grass behind them. Then when a space was burned over, the whole company moved back upon it.

"As the flames roared on toward them from the west, a little girl cried out in terror, 'Are you sure we shall not all be burned up?' The leader replied, 'My child, the flames cannot reach us here, for we are standing where the fire has been!'"[1]

As the fires of Satan's fury sweep around Israel in the last half of the Tribulation, God will move His people to a safe location and provide for her every need as He did during the wilderness wanderings. To prepare her for the evil days that will lie ahead, at the beginning of the Tribulation the Lord *admonishes* the seven churches in Asia to follow the counsel of His will, to ensure that they will be overcomers when the fires of Satan's rage are extinguished.

Wisdom says the Church, the Body of Christ, is **not** the subject of the early chapters of the *Book of Revelation.* Although this runs contrary to Church tradition, it is nevertheless the true testimony of Scripture. Both the terminology and phraseology throughout these chapters are completely foreign to Paul's Gentile epistles. However, they are frequently found in the prophetic writings. The following comparison demonstrates our point:

1. The tree of life (Gen. 3:22) cf. the tree of life (Rev. 2:7).

2. Synagogue (Mark 1:23) cf. synagogue (Rev. 2:9).

3. Balaam and Balak (Num. 23:1 cf. 31:16) cf. Balaam and Balac (Rev. 2:14).

4. He that overcometh (I John 5:4,5) cf. He that overcometh (Rev. 2:26).

5. He that hath ears to hear, let him hear (Matt. 11:15) cf. He that hath an ear, let him hear (Rev. 2:29).

6. Him shall the Son of man also confess before the angels of God (Luke 12:8) cf. I will confess His name...before His angels (Rev. 3:5).

"Unto the angel of the church of Ephesus write..." (Rev. 2:1).

One area where confusion reigns with most commentators who write on Revelation has to do with John's usage of the word *church*. They conclude that, since the Apostle John frequently uses this term, he was writing to members of the Body of Christ. However, the Greek word *ekklesia* (church) is a very general expression that more literally means "called-out ones." The context will always determine which "called-out" group is in view. Israel, for example, in time past, was called the *church* in the wilderness (Acts 7:38).

During the earthly ministry of Christ, our Lord stated that He would build His "church" on Peter's confession that He was the Christ (Messiah), the very Son of God (Matt. 16:16-18). We know that Christ came unto His own, that is, Israel, and His own received Him not (John 1:11). Consequently, He took the promise of the Kingdom and gave it to the believing remnant within the nation called the "little flock." "Fear not, little flock; for it is your Father's good pleasure **to give you the kingdom**" (Luke 12:32). These were the charter members of the Kingdom Church. On the day of Pentecost, three thousand souls were *added* to this church (Acts 2:41,47).

After the Rapture, God is going to pick up where He left off, shortly after Pentecost, when He temporarily set Israel aside in unbelief. When the prophetic program resumes in the coming Day of the Lord, the Kingdom Church will be *re-established*. The seven churches then, to whom John is writing, are seven local assemblies in Asia that are a part of the greater Kingdom Church. We must carefully distinguish between this church and the Church, the Body of Christ, of which we are members. The new entity called the *Church, which is His Body* (Col. 1:18), is only found in Paul's epistles.

ANGELS IN CHURCH

"Unto the angel of the church of Ephesus write;
These things saith He that holdeth the seven stars in
His right hand, who walketh in the midst of the seven
golden candlesticks" (Rev. 2:1).

The seven churches in Asia to which the Apostle John
was instructed to write are Ephesus, Smyrna, Pergamos,
Thyatira, Sardis, Philadelphia, and Laodicea. As we have
seen, they are Kingdom assemblies that will be established
under the ministry of the two witnesses and the 144,000.
The first local church that John addresses is at Ephesus.
Although this letter contains specific instructions for this
particular assembly, the scope of it is much broader. We believe the letters to the seven churches in Asia were meant
to be encyclical. This is confirmed by the repeated references to "the Spirit saith unto the churches" (Rev. 2:7). In
other words, these letters will be distributed for instruction among all the Kingdom assemblies, similar to Paul's
epistles today. Just as we turn to Paul's revelation for the
commands of Christ for the Church, the Tribulation saints
will turn to the Hebrew epistles for their marching orders,
with special emphasis on these seven letters.

As they used to say in days of old, "Hear ye, Hear ye:"
the *Gentile* church at Ephesus that the Apostle Paul wrote
to in his letter to the Ephesians should **not** be confused
with the *Jewish* assembly at Ephesus that John addresses.
They are two entirely different churches, being written to
at different times, by different apostles, under two different
administrations.

The Lord instructs John to write to the *angel* of the
church at Ephesus. According to the Scriptures, the angels
of God are ministers to those who are heirs of salvation
(Heb. 1:14). Under the Kingdom program, they carried on

a very active ministry among believers and often served as guardian angels. With that said, we find it highly unlikely that the Apostle John would be writing to an angel. If anything, it was the angels who made God's will known to His servants in time past, not vice versa.

The word "angel" John uses here is the Greek word *aggelos*. In the Authorized King James Version of the Bible, it is normally translated "angel," but it should be noted that it is also translated "messenger" and "messengers." As we are going to see, the term is often used of men.

For example, our Lord shared with those who sat at His feet concerning John the Baptist, that the people went out to see a prophet, but John was more than a prophet. "For this is he, of whom it is written, Behold, I send my messenger [***aggelos***] before thy face, which shall prepare thy way before thee" (Matt. 11:10). Before entering Jericho, Joshua sent out two spies on a reconnaissance mission to spy out the city. James says regarding the mission, "Likewise also was not Rahab the harlot justified by works, when she had received the messengers [***aggelos***], and had sent them out another way?" (James 2:25).

In both cases, the term *aggelos* is used in relation to men who were the servants and messengers of God. Keeping this in mind, we believe John was writing to the *pastors* of each of the churches in Asia (see Jeremiah 3:14,15). They, in turn, are to deliver the revelation to their local assemblies and make sure it is passed along to the other churches. Furthermore, it is important to note that, in John's vision, the Lord is holding the *seven stars* or messengers in His right hand, which speaks of *eternal security*. While the security of the leaders of these assemblies will be paramount, this would not be the case for the elect angels of God, whom we know to be eternal spirit beings.

THE KINGDOM GOSPEL

"I know thy works, and thy labor, and thy patience, and how thou canst not bear them which are evil: and thou hast tried them which say they are apostles, and are not, and hast found them liars: And hast borne, and hast patience, and for my name's sake hast labored, and hast not fainted. Nevertheless I have somewhat against thee, because thou hast left thy first love. Remember therefore from whence thou art fallen, and repent, and do the first works; or else I will come unto thee quickly, and will remove thy candlestick out of his place, except thou repent" (Rev. 2:2-5).

During the Olivet Discourse, the Lord revealed to the twelve apostles that "this gospel of the kingdom" they were serving under "shall be preached in all the world...and then shall the end come" (Matt. 24:14). This is the same gospel that will be proclaimed in the future Tribulation period, as John substantiates for us in Chapters 2 and 3.

The Lord says to the assembly at Ephesus, "I know thy works." This statement is found in each of the letters to the seven churches and is an integral part of the Kingdom gospel. The standing of the Church, the Body of Christ is in *grace*, but the standing of the Kingdom Church is rooted in *works*. These works include circumcision, repentance, water baptism, keeping the Sabbath, etc.

It is essential to remember that in the Tribulation, Israel, nationally, will again be the channel of God's blessing; she will be the apple of His eye. Since she had a *covenant relationship* with God, it will be necessary at that day to call her again to repentance. Today the Body of Christ is only made up of believers who have placed their faith in Christ. Conversely, the chosen nation of Israel was, and will be in the future, made up of both believers and unbelievers (Luke 3:7-9 cf. Rom. 9:6,7). Therefore, the theme of

Christ's message to each of the seven churches in Asia is "repentance" and the necessity for those within these assemblies to exhibit the "fruits of repentance" (Luke 3:8).

According to John the Baptist, these "fruits of repentance" included providing for the poor. If an Israelite had two coats, he was to give to someone who didn't have a coat. If a man had food on his table, he was to share it with his neighbor who had none. We should pause here a moment to say that the importance of these things cannot be overstated, seeing that many will be driven from their homes and livelihoods due to persecution in that day.

Those who collected money for the powers-that-be were not to charge more than what was owed. In accordance with Israel's covenant relationship, the law said, "Thou shalt not steal." Soldiers were not to take advantage of the people by falsely accusing them, for the law said, "Thou shalt not bear false witness." Essentially, the Lord is calling attention to the assembly's selfishness at Ephesus. These are some of the "first works" the Lord speaks of in Revelation 2:5 whereby the assembly could be *restored* to her "first love." Because Israel is the future bride of Christ, He is her first love, but some within the seven assemblies had inadvertently drifted away from Him due to the cares of this life (John 3:28-30 cf. Rev. 19:7,8). Failure to repent would have serious consequences—namely, the loss of the Lord's blessing.

The Lord also commends this assembly for their stand against evil and workers of evil. He points out how they could "not bear them which are evil: and thou hast tried them which say they are apostles, and are not, and hast found them liars" (Rev. 2:2). Judgment under the Kingdom gospel was swift and sure. An example is found in the account of Ananias and Sapphira, who sold a piece of land

and brought the proceeds and laid them at the feet of the apostles. The problem was that they withheld some of the money for themselves. Peter exposed the evil deed and how they had lied to God. The end result was they were both pronounced dead at the scene (Acts 5:1-11).

Of course, today there are no apostles; the office has been completely vacated by God. Interestingly, after the Rapture, the office of apostle will again be filled, which is implied by the fact that there will be false apostles who will be exposed for their evil deeds. The true apostles of God in the coming Day of the Lord, like Peter, will have the authority to pronounce judgment under the guidelines of the Kingdom gospel.

> "But this thou hast, that thou hatest the deeds of
> the Nicolaitanes, which I also hate" (Rev. 2:6).

Historically, there is no evidence whatsoever that there was ever a sect called the Nicolaitanes in biblical times. The name Nicolaitanes means, "destruction of the people." Apparently it is some sort of religious sect in the future Tribulation that will be tied to the one-world church (Rev. 17:1-7). The apostate church will be bent on corrupting and destroying the Kingdom Church through the deeds of the Nicolaitanes, the doctrine of Balaam, and the seduction of Jezebel, as we will see. One thing we know for certain; The Lord *hates* the deeds and the doctrine of the Nicolaitanes. It is always good to hate what the Lord hates, which will be true of the Kingdom believers at Ephesus.

THE PARADISE OF GOD

> "He that hath an ear, let him hear what the Spirit
> saith unto the churches; To him that overcometh will
> I give to eat of the tree of life, which is in the midst of
> the paradise of God" (Rev. 2:7).

Only those who are born again in that day will have spiritual ears to hear and receive what the Spirit teaches. The overcomers are those who have submitted themselves to their first love. They are those who continue in the "first works" and deplore evil and love righteousness. To them it is promised that they will partake of the *Tree of Life*, at which time they will receive life and life eternal. What the Kingdom saints are promised here we already have in Christ.

In the beginning, God placed the Tree of Life in the Garden of Eden. After Adam and Eve sinned, the Lord posted Cherubim around it with a flaming sword to ensure that no one partook of it. Had Adam and Eve done so in their fallen state, they would have lived eternally in a sinful state without the hope of redemption (Gen. 3:22). Shortly after the fall, God removed paradise from Eden and placed it in *hades*, located in the center of the earth (Luke 16:23-25; 23:43 cf. Eph. 4:8-10). After Calvary, Christ removed it from the earth, placing it in the third heaven where it remains to this day (II Cor. 12:1-4). While we are not told, paradise and the Tree of Life will probably be returned to the earth during the millennial reign of Christ, seeing that the curse will be partially lifted. We know for certain the Tree of Life will be a part of the new earth throughout eternity (Rev. 22:1-7).

By way of application, there are a number of things we can glean for our benefit from the Lord's instructions to the Kingdom saints. First and foremost, we too must guard against drifting away from our "first love." The cares and responsibilities of this world can rob us of the joy we once had when we first trusted Christ. After our conversion, we couldn't wait to learn more about Him and be in the company of those who love Him, but the years all too often dull our spiritual senses. Perhaps we each need to pause a moment and ask, have I wandered from my first love?

The Lord commended the future Kingdom believers for their hatred of evil and for openly exposing those who taught unsound doctrine. Can the same be said of us today? Do we hate evil with the same passion as they will, or do we tolerate it? When faced with unsound teaching, do we confront it or are we more inclined to look the other way out of fear we might offend someone? May the Lord give us the resolve to hate what He hates and love what He loves, for His honor and glory.

THE JEWISH ASSEMBLY AT SMYRNA

"And unto the angel of the church in Smyrna write; These things saith the first and the last, which was dead, and is alive" (Rev. 2:8).

As the Apostle John stood on the balcony, as it were, overlooking the events of the future Tribulation period, next he was instructed to write to the pastor of the church in Smyrna. Even though this message from the Lord is primarily meant for this assembly, once again, it is also intended for the other churches in Asia Minor who will experience many of the same things (Rev. 2:17a).

It is noteworthy that the name *Smyrna* means "myrrh, a bitter, but fragrant perfume with which they embalmed the dead" in biblical times. You will recall how Joseph and Nicodemus used myrrh and aloes when they prepared our Lord's body for burial after His crucifixion; they did so in accordance with Jewish burial customs (John 19:38-40). So the name *Smyrna* is closely associated with death! It is also important to keep in mind how the priests in the Old Testament were instructed to include *myrrh* (stacte) as one of the ingredients that made up the incense they burned on the golden altar of incense, which was well pleasing to the LORD (Ex. 30:34-38). More on this in a moment!

In the introductory remarks to each of the seven churches, John begins with a statement that the Son of Man made in chapter one when He was standing in the midst of the assemblies. Each statement perfectly fits the church to whom it was made, as we see below.

Admonition

Vision of the Son of Man:

"And I turned to see the voice that spake with me. And being turned, I saw seven golden candlesticks; And in the midst of the seven candlesticks one like unto the Son of man" (Rev. 1:12,13).

To Ephesus:

"These things saith He...who walketh in the midst of the seven golden candlesticks" (Rev. 2:1).

"Nevertheless I have somewhat against thee, because thou hast left thy first love. Remember therefore from whence thou art fallen, and repent, and do the first works; or else I will come unto thee quickly, and will remove thy candlestick out of his place" (Rev. 2:4,5).

Martyrdom

Vision of the Son of Man:

"I am He that liveth, and was dead; and, behold, I am alive for evermore, Amen; and have the keys of hell [*hades*] and of death" (Rev. 1:18).

To Smyrna:

"These things saith the first and the last, which was dead, and is alive" (Rev. 2:8b).

"Be thou faithful unto death, and I will give thee a crown of life" (Rev. 2:10b).

Chastisement

Vision of the Son of Man:

"And out of His mouth went a sharp twoedged sword" (Rev. 1:16).

To Pergamos:

"These things saith He which hath the sharp sword with two edges" (Rev. 2:12b).

"Repent; or else I will come unto thee quickly, and will fight against them with the sword of my mouth" (Rev. 2:16).

Judgment

Vision of the Son of Man:

"And His eyes were as a flame of fire; And His feet like unto fine brass, as if they burned in a furnace" (Rev. 1:14b,15a).

To Thyatira:

"These things saith the Son of God, who hath His eyes like unto a flame of fire, and His feet are like fine brass" (Rev. 2:18).

"And I will kill her children [unbelieving followers of Jezebel] with death; and all the churches shall know that I am He which searcheth the reins and hearts: and I will give unto every one of you according to your works" (Rev. 2:23).

Security

Vision of the Son of Man:

"...from Him...and from the seven Spirits which are before His throne...for ever and ever. Amen. ...And He had in His right hand seven stars...The seven stars are the angels of the seven churches..." (Rev. 1:4,6,16,20).

To Sardis:

> "These things saith He that hath the seven Spirits of God [special class of angels], and the seven stars [seven ministers of the gospel of the Kingdom]" (Rev. 3:1).

> "He that overcometh, the same shall be clothed in white raiment; and I will not blot out his name out of the book of life, but I will confess his name before my Father, and before His angels" (Rev. 3:5).

Eternal Kingdom

Vision of the Son of Man:

> "I am He that liveth, and was dead; and, behold, I am alive for evermore, Amen; and have the keys of hell [hades] and of death" (Rev. 1:18).

To Philadelphia:

> "These things saith He that is holy, He that is true, He that hath the key of David, He that openeth, and no man shutteth; and shutteth, and no man openeth" (Rev. 3:7).

> "Him that overcometh will I make a pillar in the temple of my God, and he shall go no more out: and I will write upon him the name of my God, and the name of the city of my God, which is new Jerusalem, which cometh down out of heaven from my God" (Rev. 3:12).

The Judge

Vision of the Son of Man:

> "And from Jesus Christ, who is the faithful witness" (Rev. 1:5a).

To Laodicea:

> "These things saith the Amen, the faithful and true witness, the beginning of the creation of God" (Rev. 3:14).

"Behold, I stand at the door, and knock [as Judge—
James 5:9]: if any man hear my voice, and open the
door, I will come in to him, and will sup with him, and
he with me" (Rev. 3:20).

TRUSTING GOD IN TRYING TIMES

"On his march through Asia Minor, Alexander [the
Great] fell dangerously ill. His physicians were afraid to
treat him because if they did not succeed, the Macedonian
army would suspect them of malpractice [the consequence
of which would have been death]. Only one, Philip the Acar-
nanian, was willing to take the risk, as he had confidence in
both the king's friendship and his own drugs.

"While the medicine was being prepared, Alexander
received a letter from an enemy of Philip's that accused
the physician of having been bribed by the Persian king to
poison his master. Alexander read the letter and slipped
it under his pillow without showing it to anyone. When
Philip entered the tent with the medicine, Alexander took
the cup from him, at the same time handing Philip the letter. While the physician was reading it, Alexander calmly
drank the contents of the cup. Horrified and indignant at
the calumny [malicious misrepresentation], Philip threw
himself down at the king's bedside, but Alexander assured
him that he had complete confidence in his honor. After
three days the king was well enough to appear again before
his army."[2]

If men place this type of confidence in one another, which
is commendable, how much more should it be true in the
affairs of God, especially when we consider what lies ahead
for those who enter the coming Tribulation. Those times
will require *total* trust and dependence on God, as we are
going to witness.

> "I know thy works, and tribulation, and poverty, (but thou art rich) and I know the blasphemy of them which say they are Jews, and are not, but are the synagogue of Satan" (Rev. 2:9).

Here the Lord acknowledges the *works* of this assembly, which are many and varied under the Kingdom gospel. One such requirement will be to keep the *Sabbath* faithfully. In fact, the Lord instructed those who would endure the coming Day of the Lord that they are to pray that the abomination of desolation does not take place on the Sabbath (Matt. 24:15-20).

The "abomination of desolation" is when the Antichrist enters the temple in Jerusalem and declares himself to be God. When they witness this unsettling event, they are to flee to the mountains. The problem is that a Sabbath day's journey was a little less than a mile, which, of course, would not be far enough to get out of harm's way. This particular event will mark the beginning of a great holocaust in Israel, as the pursuing death machine of the Antichrist sweeps across the land. This is why they are to pray that their flight be not on the Sabbath.

The faithful at Smyrna will also suffer *tribulation* and *poverty*, which will be commonplace in that day. To openly name the name of Christ in the future Tribulation will cost many their livelihoods. Additionally, under the third seal judgment, the demonic rider of the black horse will bring *famine* to the earth, so much so that it will take nearly an entire day's wages to purchase a couple loaves of bread (Rev. 6:5,6).

As the time of Jacob's Trouble intensifies, the Antichrist will require the mark of the beast. Without this mark, no one will be able to buy or sell; however, those who do receive it will be eternally damned (Rev. 13:16-18 cf. 14:9-11).

69

Those believers who somehow escaped *poverty* up to this point will be plunged into it practically overnight. Mercifully, God will providentially intervene on behalf of His people and supernaturally provide for them as He did during the wilderness wanderings. They will literally pray in that day, "Give us this day our daily bread," in fulfillment of the Lord's prayer. Thanks be to God that we are living in the Dispensation of Grace and will never encounter the mark of the beast.

In view of the persecutions and poverty these Kingdom saints will suffer at Smyrna, the Lord reminds them, "but thou art rich." Rich, you see, because they were *laying up treasures* in heaven, "where neither moth nor rust doth corrupt, and where thieves do not break through nor steal" (Matt. 6:20). For their faithful service in keeping the commandments of God and taking a stand for Christ, they will be richly rewarded in the coming Kingdom when the Son of Man sits on the throne of His glory.

To add insult to injury, the Lord reveals here that the saints at Smyrna will also suffer at the hands of their own countrymen, as He did. "And I know the blasphemy of them which say they are Jews, and are not, but are the synagogue of Satan." Once again, it is very important to remember, and remember well, that unlike the Body of Christ, Israel, nationally, will *again* be made up of believers and unbelievers, as this passage clearly teaches.

This looks back to the parable of the wheat and tares. The "tares" made reference to in the parable "are the children of the wicked one" (Matt. 13:38). This phraseology is never used of unbelievers in general, but is reserved for a specific group known as *religious* unbelievers (John 8:38-44). In time past, these "tares" were the religious Pharisees, Sadducees, scribes, and hypocrites who themselves will never enter the

Kingdom, and yet, due to their self-righteous requirements, barred the way for others to enter (Luke 11:52). They piously made long prayers in the houses of widows, hoping to receive gifts to fill their coffers. These workers of the evil one would travel great distances to win one proselyte to their religious system and "make him twofold more the child of hell" than themselves (Matt. 23:13-15).

There will be a similar group of Jewish religious leaders and their followers at Smyrna who will deceive the unsuspecting and oppress those who place their faith in the Messiah. The Lord exposes them as those who are of the *synagogue of Satan* and, near the end of His earthly ministry He predicted the following: "They shall put you out of the synagogues: yea, the time cometh, that whosoever killeth you will think that he doeth God service" (John 16:2).

MARTYRDOM

"Fear none of those things which thou shalt suffer: behold, the devil shall cast some of you into prison, that ye may be tried; and ye shall have tribulation ten days: be thou faithful unto death, and I will give thee a crown of life" (Rev. 2:10).

During the time of Christ, when the Lord was ministering upon the earth, Satan opposed the advancement of the Kingdom gospel by instigating brutal acts of torture, imprisonments, martyrdom, demonization, persecutions, etc. Today, Christ is carrying out His heavenly ministry to the Church; consequently, the members of the Body of Christ are engaged in a spiritual warfare against spiritual wickedness in heavenly places. The theater of warfare today is a battle for the mind (Eph. 6:11-18).

After the Rapture, this warfare will revert back to earth due to the fact that Christ is going to overthrow the kingdom of Satan in the coming Tribulation and establish His Kingdom of Righteousness. Knowing that his time is short, the adversary will pull out all the stops again to hinder the advancement of the gospel of the Kingdom. The attacks that took place during the time of Christ are going to pale in comparison when Satan unleashes his fury on these future Kingdom saints, as the chapters that follow in the Apocalypse clearly indicate.

The Lord reveals to the saints at Smyrna that some of their number will go through a fiery trial. Satan will be instrumental in causing an uprising against them resulting, in their imprisonment for a period of "ten days," during which time their faith will be tested. Some interpret these ten days to be symbolic of the supposed ten years of persecution under Roman Emperor Diocletian beginning in 284 A.D.; however, there is no credible evidence whatsoever that this was the case. Even if this were true, the persecution would have been of the Church, the Body of Christ, not the Kingdom Church, that is under consideration in this passage.

We are always to take a literal interpretation of the Scriptures unless the context demands otherwise. There is no reason to believe that we are to take the ten days to be anything other than ten literal days. It is merely a prediction of things to come.

Of course, we are reminded of a related period of time in the life of Daniel when he endured a similar trial. When King Nebuchadnezzar conquered Israel, he returned to Babylon, bringing with him the spoils of victory, which included those of the captivity to serve in his kingdom. Old Nebuchadnezzar took the best and the brightest of those he captured to stand in his court, four of whom were Daniel, Shadrach, Meshach, and Abednego. These subjects were taught the knowledge and language of the Chaldeans so they could serve the king as advisors. To ensure these Hebrew children developed properly, the king ordered that they be given a portion of his food and drink.

> "But Daniel purposed in his heart that he would not defile himself with the portion of the king's meat, nor with the wine which he drank" (Dan. 1:8a).

In addition to the king's food being unclean according to the Law of Moses, at least for the most part, it also had been offered to idols before being given to Daniel to eat. This set in motion a fiery trial for the young Hebrew who *refused* to compromise his faith. Daniel's refusal to partake of the king's portion placed not only his life in danger, but also the life of the prince of the eunuchs whom Nebuchadnezzar had placed over the Hebrew children. If those Hebrew children weren't well nourished when they stood before the king, heads could roll, literally!

Daniel requested of the overseer Melzar that he and his companions be permitted to eat vegetables and drink water for *ten days* to demonstrate that they would do as well or better on this diet than they would do eating the king's portion (Dan. 1:11-16). After ten days, the Hebrew children passed the test and were fairer and fatter than their counterparts who ate the king's food.

Daniel trusted that God would provide a way of deliverance; this will also be true of the future Tribulation saints at Smyrna, but with a completely different outcome. In their case, they are to be "faithful unto death," but thankfully the Lord adds the promise: "And I will give thee a crown of life." These instructions are totally foreign to the Body of Christ because Paul tells us to "present [our] bodies a **living** sacrifice, holy, acceptable unto God, which is [our] reasonable service" (Rom. 12:1).

In contrast, many of these Kingdom saints are going to suffer *martyrdom* for the cause of Christ, because they loved not their lives even unto death. These are some of the souls that the Apostle John saw in the fifth seal who "were slain for the Word of God, and for the testimony which they held" (Rev. 6:9). This church is properly named, seeing that Smyrna, as we have noted, means *myrrh*, that bittersweet fragrance that was well pleasing to the Lord. Hence, "Precious in the sight of the Lord is the death of His saints" (Psa. 116:15).

The deliverance for these martyrs who trust God will come in the first resurrection, when they are raised from the dead to enter into the blessings of the Kingdom. This *hope* is based on the Lord's opening statement to this assembly, that He is "the first and the last, **which was dead, and is alive**" (Rev. 2:8). In other words, Christ conquered death and rose again; as a result, He has promised these martyrs who place their trust in Him that they too will be raised at the last day. The *crown of life*, then, is a resurrected life that is forevermore!

> "He that hath an ear, let him hear what the Spirit saith unto the churches; He that overcometh shall not be hurt of the second death" (Rev. 2:11).

Deception will be a powerful tool of Satan in the coming Tribulation, which will make it extremely difficult to discern who is saved and who is counterfeit, especially since they will be operating under a performance-based system (Matt. 7:21-23). Only the *overcomers* will escape the second death. According to the Scriptures, the *second death* is eternal separation from God in the Lake of Fire (II Thes. 1:7-9 cf. Rev. 20:14,15). But who are these overcomers? The Apostle John reveals for us in his writings that they are those who are **born again**—those who believe Jesus Christ is the Son of God!

"For whatsoever is born of God overcometh the world: and this is the victory that overcometh the world, even our faith. Who is he that overcometh the world, but he that *believeth* that Jesus is the Son of God?" (I John 5:4,5).

The churches at Ephesus and Smyrna heeded the warnings of God, for which they are commended, but will the same be true of the remainder of these assemblies? Many ministers of the gospel today are willing to raise a faded flag or no flag at all for fear of offending someone, but they do so at the peril of those who have been placed in their care. We raise before you a red flag to challenge you to heed the warnings of God found in Paul's epistles (see I Cor. 10:1-15). The Lord has placed them in His Word for our benefit. While we are not under God's judgment for our sins because of the finished work of Christ, we are not beyond suffering loss at the Judgment Seat of Christ if we fail to take these warnings seriously.

4

The Kingdom Church at Pergamos and Thyatira

"What thou seest, write in a book, and send it unto the seven churches which are in Asia; unto Ephesus, and unto Smyrna, and unto Pergamos, and unto Thyatira, and unto Sardis, and unto Philadelphia, and unto Laodicea."

—Revelation 1:11

THE JEWISH ASSEMBLY AT PERGAMOS

"And to the angel of the church in Pergamos write; These things saith He which hath the sharp sword with two edges" (Rev. 2:12).

It is important to remember throughout our study of the *Book of Revelation* that the Apostle John was caught away in the Spirit to the future Day of the Lord. This conclusion is based on the apostle's own words found in Revelation 1:9,10. When John addresses the seven churches in Asia he is not looking back over seven successive periods of Church history, as some claim. With the precision of a Global Positioning System, the apostle's narrative is pointing the reader in the opposite direction.

Remember those days of the old video recorders when you could fast forward the tape to watch the end of a movie or documentary? Essentially, the Spirit of God fast-forwarded time and placed John in the period called Jacob's Trouble so he could record the events of the End Time. Sound farfetched? It isn't to the eye of faith, for what is prophecy, but history written in advance?

THE THRONE OF SATAN

The next church John was instructed to address is Pergamos, the name of which means, roughly, a fortified tower. This is fitting because Pergamos is where Satan will establish his throne and actually dwell as he aspires to "ascend above the heights of the clouds" and "be like the most High" (Isa. 14:12-14).

> "I know thy works, and where thou dwellest, even where Satan's seat [throne] is: and thou holdest fast my name, and hast not denied my faith" (Rev. 2:13a).

Through the centuries, the popular notion has been that Satan is confined to Hell where he reigns supreme and has his sphere of influence. While it is true that this everlasting fire was created for the devil and his angels, Satan has yet to set foot there. Once he is confined to Hell at the Great White Throne Judgment, he will not have the freedom ever again to roam the earth or the heavens as we see him doing here at Pergamos.

Satan's power and realm of influence must never be underestimated; he is the god of this world (II Cor. 4:4). Interestingly, the Scriptures never deny these things or question his authority over the kingdoms of this world. This is clearly seen when he tempted our Lord.

> "Again, the devil taketh Him up into an exceeding high mountain, and showeth Him all the kingdoms of the world, and the glory of them; And saith unto Him, All these things will I give thee, if thou wilt fall down and worship me" (Matt. 4:8,9).
>
> "And the devil said unto Him, All this power will I give thee, and the glory of them: for that is delivered unto me; and to whomsoever I will I give it" (Luke 4:6).

Notice the devil states that the kingdoms of this world were "delivered to him." In the Garden of Eden, when Adam sinned against God, he handed over the dominion of all the earth, which was rightfully his, to Satan. Obviously, the devil had to have control of these realms to be in a position to offer them and the glory of them to tempt the Lord. Until the Lord returns, Satan is the one who is pulling all the strings behind the scenes in the affairs of men.

So we are to understand that Satan isn't stoking the fires of Hell or confined there, as much as he delights that men think this to be the case. While his base of operations is the second heaven, he still has access to the earth, as he did in the days of Job. When the Lord resumes His earthly ministry in the coming Tribulation, Satan is going to set up a branch office in the city of Pergamos from which he will ruthlessly attack the Kingdom churches. Satan not only wants to ascend on high to be like God, he also desires to reign on the earth in Christ's stead. He wants it all!

Many seem to believe that Satan and his workers of darkness spend all their time in taverns, casinos, drug houses, and brothels. In reality, those who frequent such places have *willingly* given themselves over to the evil one. He simply opened the door of these establishments and the lust of the flesh took over from there. If there is one passion that Satan has more than any other, it is to destroy the plans and purposes of God. In his obsession to accomplish this goal, Satan sends out his ministers who transform themselves to appear as ministers of righteousness, who then corrupt the Word of God and deceive the unwary with false teaching.

It is sad that many in a local assembly such as we have here at Pergamos are blindsided by Satan's subtlety. To those who aren't taken in by the schemes of the devil, the

Lord says, "I know thy works...and thou holdest fast my name, and hast not denied my faith." During the Tribulation, the name of Christ will be blasphemed by those who align themselves with the exploits of Satan (Rev. 13:6). To call His name into question is to deny He is the Messiah, the very Son of God (John 20:31).

The Lord will be well pleased with those at Pergamos who believe that He is who He claims to be, and with their holding fast to the truth that He is God. Therefore they will refuse the mark of the beast or the number of his name (Rev. 13:17,18). They are also commended for not denying His faith, an obvious reference to the Kingdom gospel which includes the faithfulness of Christ to provide redemption for His people (Matt. 24:14; Luke 1:68,69 cf. Rev. 14:12).

> "Even in those days wherein Antipas was my faithful martyr, who was slain among you, where Satan dwelleth" (Rev. 2:13b).

We must bear in mind that, when John is writing to the seven churches in Asia, the Tribulation period is well underway and many dear saints will have already suffered martyrdom, one of whom is Antipas. One will search in vain to find any *credible* historical references to a man by the name of Antipas, who was martyred at Pergamos in John's day. This is passing strange, seeing that he is such a prominent figure. To those who are sure to argue, "But tradition says..," please see Mark 7:13. Once again, the Apostle John isn't looking back to the Church, the Body of Christ, but forward to a future day.

We have a number of examples in the prophetic Scriptures where a prominent figure who was to play a key role in the plans and purposes of God was named years before he was born. We believe this is the case with Antipas. For example, in the days of Jeroboam, God sent a prophet from

Judah who delivered the following prophecy regarding the coming of a Reformer: "Behold, a child shall be born unto the house of David, **Josiah by name**..." (I Kings 13:1-3 cf. II Kings 22:1,2). This prophecy was given approximately three centuries before Josiah's birth.

Similarly, Isaiah gave the name of the future king of Persia nearly two centuries before he stepped onto the stage of the world. The Lord revealed to the prophet: "That saith of **Cyrus**, He is my shepherd, and shall perform all my pleasure: even saying to Jerusalem, thou shalt be built; and to the temple, thy foundation shall be laid" (Isa. 44:28 cf. II Chron. 36:22).

THE DANGER OF COMPROMISE

The story is told "of a Russian named Ivanovich who visited the Moscow Zoo for the first time. To his amazement he found a little lamb sharing the cage that held a big fierce bear. Ivanovich expressed surprise to his communist guide. The guide smiled and said, 'That is peaceful coexistence.' When Ivanovich doubtfully shook his head, the guide reluctantly went on to explain 'Of course, we have to put in a fresh lamb every morning.' You see peaceful coexistence between right and wrong, God and the devil is not possible. You must learn to whom to say 'No.'"[1]

How true! Nothing will undermine the Lord's work more quickly than *compromise*. It is an insidious mood of toleration of unsound teaching for the sake of peaceful coexistence. Mark these words and mark them well: Compromise is the influence of Satan to corrupt the Word of God! It is a shame that Satan so often uses believers to accomplish his purpose. Essentially, there will be three groups that make up the assembly at Pergamos: those who defend the faith, those who compromise it, and those who deny it. The Lord

singles out the second group who are all too willing to tolerate the unsound teachings of Balaam and the Nicolaitanes
in their midst.

> "But I have a few things against thee, because thou
> hast there them that hold the doctrine of Balaam, who
> taught Balac to cast a stumblingblock before the chil-
> dren of Israel, to eat things sacrificed unto idols, and to
> commit fornication. So hast thou also them that hold
> the doctrine of the Nicolaitanes, which thing I hate"
> (Rev. 2:14,15).

What exactly is Balaamism? Balaam was a hireling
prophet who sought to *market* his gift. This is the *way of
Balaam*. When Balak, the king of the Moabites, saw how
the Amorites were utterly destroyed by the children of Israel, he feared that he was going to suffer the same fate. So
he sent the elders of Moab with gifts to Balaam, hoping he
would be persuaded to curse Israel. Balak reasoned that if
the prophet cursed the chosen nation, he would prevail and
drive her out of the land.

The very fact that these bearers of silver and gold were
sent to Balaam strongly suggests that the reputation of
the prophet preceded him. As they say, money talks, and
Balaam was listening. But God would not allow the prophet
to return with the elders of Moab, nor did He permit him
to curse Israel. However, temptation always knocks at the
door of opportunity more than once, so it should not surprise us when the princes of Moab returned to offer Balaam
riches untold and even greater honor throughout the realm.
Rather than accept the will of God regarding the matter, he
approached the face of the Lord again. Balaam reasoned
that, since Israel had sinned against God, she deserved to be
cursed, which, of course, meant he would reap a handsome
sum for his effort. He had no concern whatsoever for others,

that many of them would perish, as long as it profited him. This time God gave Balaam the liberty to go, as a *test*. This shows the true intent of Balaam's heart, seeing that he fully understood it was not God's will for him to go; he went nevertheless. Lust filled his heart!

Amazingly, Balaam's journey was interrupted when the ass upon which he was riding saw the Angel of the LORD standing in the way with a sword drawn. Although the money-blinded prophet could not see the Angel of the LORD at first, the ass did and turned aside into the field. The second time Balaam tried to drive the ass onward, she crushed his foot against the wall. The third time she saw the Angel of the LORD, she collapsed beneath the prophet. Each time, Balaam beat the beast of burden unmercifully, but after the third beating, the ass spoke to him (See Numbers 22). Now that would leave you speechless!

The Lord often uses unique ways to get our attention, but in this case we must also remember that nothing is impossible with God (Jer. 32:17 cf. Luke 1:37). We are to see it was according to God's purpose that Balaam "was rebuked for his iniquity: the dumb ass speaking with man's voice forbad the madness of the prophet" (II Pet. 2:16). Then the LORD opened his eyes and Balaam saw the Angel of the LORD standing in the way. It is important to note that this was a pre-incarnate appearance of Christ, the very One who would redeem Israel from the curse of the law. This was the *error of Balaam* (Jude 11). He reasoned that a holy God must curse Israel on the basis of His righteousness. But the hireling prophet failed to understand the higher purpose of God to redeem Israel at the Cross, where Christ would be made a curse for the sins of His people (Gal. 3:13). Consequently, the Lord rebuked the wayward prophet: "Behold, I went out to withstand thee, because thy way is perverse before me" (Num. 22:32).

After Balaam realized God would not allow him to curse Israel, he *deceitfully* devised a plan to corrupt Israel. He taught Balak to entice the chosen nation into eating things that had been offered to idols and to commit fornication, both of which were strictly forbidden by God. This is the *doctrine of Balaam* made reference to here in Revelation 2:14. Israel was only to worship the true and living God. She was to be a *separate* nation unto God; therefore, she was not to marry those of other nations. So when the Israelites committed fornication with the pagan daughters of Moab, God sent a plague among His people wherein 24,000 perished (Num. 25:1-9).

The false teachers at Pergamos were promoting the *doctrine of Balaam*, which is to say that they were imitating the prophet. Balaamism is a system of teaching that's based purely upon human reasoning. It is worldliness in its worst forms: lust, immorality, greed, and personal advancement at the expense of others. The face of evil may change, but its devastating effects are always the same.

The history of Israel will repeat itself in the Day of the Lord when she will commit the same errors as in the past. Those at Pergamos who compromise the faith will tolerate *idolatry* and *immorality*, probably convincing themselves that everyone's doing it. The thinking will be, "Let's be open-minded," which will play perfectly into Satan's hand. Add to this the doctrine of the Nicolaitans, where a hierarchy is placed over the Lord's people, to lord over them, and you have the following response from the Lord:

> "Repent; or else I will come unto thee quickly, and will fight against them with the sword of my mouth. He that hath an ear, let him hear what the Spirit saith unto the churches" (Rev. 2:16,17a).

When the Lord calls this assembly to repentance, He is primarily addressing those who are guilty of compromising the faith. They are to have a change of heart, mind, and direction in their involvement in and toleration of promiscuity. Their idea of "progressive thinking" is met head on by the Lord's warning that if they do not turn from their evil ways, He will "come...quickly." This is not a reference to Christ's Second Coming, but to the Lord unexpectedly visiting them, as He did Balaam in the way.

He Who has "the sharp sword with two edges" (v. 12), which pierces through the very intent of the heart, will fight against them with the sword of His mouth. In other words, the Lord will *chastise* them, if they fail to repent, with the sole purpose of restoring them to the faith. "My son, despise not thou the chastening of the Lord, nor faint when thou art rebuked of Him: For whom the Lord loveth He chasteneth, and scourgeth every son whom He receiveth" (Heb. 12:5,6). Those who choose to continue in their rebellion after being chastened will undoubtedly suffer the loss of the Lord's blessing. The Lord will take up the matter with them again at the beginning of the Millennium when He judges Israel and the nations. Great will be their loss!

THE REWARDS OF OBEDIENCE

> "To him that overcometh will I give to eat of the hidden manna, and will give him a white stone, and in the stone a new name written, which no man knoweth saving he that receiveth it" (Rev. 2:17).

If there is one term that stands out more than any other in the letters to the seven churches, it is the term *overcometh*. In fact, the term *overcometh* (Gr. *nikao*) appears 16 times throughout the Book of Revelation, nine of which appear in John's letters to the churches in Asia.

On the other hand, this particular word is found just twice in Paul's epistles, but only once in relation to the Gentiles, and for good reason. As members of the Body of Christ we are more than conquerors in Him. We are to understand, as members of His Body, that we are *already* overcomers in Christ (Rom. 8:35-39; Col. 2:10).

While we know that the true, post-Rapture believer will be an overcomer in the future Tribulation, they won't enjoy the assurance of their salvation as we do. They will always wonder if they have done enough to please the Lord; consequently, they are instructed to "endure to the end" (Matt. 10:22; 24:13; Mark 13:13), to be overcomers, etc.

The reward for overcoming is to eat of the hidden manna. I think most Israelites from the time they've been knee-high to a grasshopper understand the significance of this statement. In the Old Testament, Aaron placed a golden pot of manna (hidden away, incorruptible) in the Ark of the Covenant, alongside the tablets of stone and his rod. It was to be a constant reminder to the chosen nation throughout her generations of how God had made a daily provision for her in the wilderness (Ex. 16:33 cf. Heb. 9:4). Christ is the hidden manna, who is seated at the right hand of the Father, out of view, until all His enemies are made His footstool. He is the spiritual provision these overcomers will partake of in the coming Kingdom (John 6:51). He is the Bread of life! In that day, they will partake of His righteousness and His peace, and receive the forgiveness of their sins (Acts 3:19). What they are promised, we *already* possess in Christ, by grace!

The promise of the Lord to give the overcomer "a white stone, and in the stone a new name written," is also the subject of the prophetic Scriptures. Names, of course, are used to distinguish one person from another. In biblical times, they also had great significance attached to them. For example, after 400 years of silence, which was an indication of God's displeasure with His people, we are introduced to

Zacharias and Elizabeth in the first chapter of the Gospel according to Luke. Zacharias means "Jehovah has remembered," while Elizabeth means "God's oath." When we combine the two names, we have, "God has remembered His oath." In short, God had not forgotten His people; He would honor His promise that He originally gave to Abraham.

The Lord occasionally assigned *new names* in time past. He changed Jacob's name, which means "deceiver," to *Israel*, which means "a prince with God." The new name, Israel, more accurately described his calling and relationship with God. The same will be true when those who overcome the Antichrist are given new names, known only to them, that will be inscribed on white gemstones. It, too, will express some characteristic of their devotion to Christ. The Lord also says this about those who fear Him and give thought to His name: "And they shall be mine, saith the LORD of hosts, in that day when I make up my jewels; and I will spare them, as a man spareth his own son that serveth him" (Mal. 3:17).

It has been correctly said, "In the *manna* we see the appreciation of Christ by the saint, but in the *white stone* the appreciation of the saint by Christ."[1]

SOMETHING TO THINK ABOUT!

By way of practical application, Satan is using the same strategy today to destroy the testimony of members of the Body of Christ through immorality. Whatever form fornication may take, whether it is premarital sex, adultery, incest, homosexuality, sensuality, or pornography, it is a very effective tool of the evil one. As Paul says regarding Satan, "we are not ignorant of his devices." It is sad to say that many seem to be ignorant of them these days, or is it that they are *willingly* ignorant? "A wise man feareth, and departeth from evil: but the fool rageth, and is confident" (Prov. 14:16).

Another way in which Satan has done his work well is by subtly influencing believers to sacrifice their convictions on the altar of compromise. Dear ones, compromise is a cancer. It is a mood of toleration that promises *acceptance* at the expense of the gospel of the grace of God. It is a slippery slope that will cause you eventually to lose your identity as a grace believer. The same can be true of a local grace assembly if the leadership is more interested in numbers than standing for the truth. Beware!

THE JEWISH ASSEMBLY AT THYATIRA

"And unto the angel of the church in Thyatira write; These things saith the Son of God, who hath His eyes like unto a flame of fire, and His feet are like fine brass" (Rev. 2:18).

John is now instructed to turn his attention to the church at Thyatira. Of course, Lydia, who was from Thyatira, is often credited with establishing this local Jewish assembly. But there are two major problems with this conclusion.

First, Lydia (Gentile name) was saved under Paul's gospel; therefore, if she was instrumental in helping start an assembly in this city, of which there is no evidence, it would have been made up of members of the Body of Christ. We know, however, John was writing to *Kingdom saints* in the coming Day of the Lord.

Second, there is no historical record that a local Kingdom Church ever existed at Thyatira in biblical times. Robert Brock makes this insightful comment in his writings:

"When the Bible was being formed into one book by the early Church Fathers, many of them thought that the Book of Revelation should not be included in the canon of

Scripture. The authorship of John was disputed, and one of the major reasons was the message to the church at Thyatira. THERE WAS NO CHURCH IN EXISTENCE AT THYATIRA AT THAT TIME...."²

THE CONFLICT OF THE AGES

This is a fitting title, originally coined by James M. Gray, to describe Satan's opposition to the plans and purpose of God in redemption. The conflict began when man disobeyed God and fell into sin, which brought with it the promise of a coming Redeemer (Gen. 3:15). From that day forward, Satan would do everything in his power to destroy the bloodline that would give rise to the Seed of the woman, whom we know to be the Redeemer.

With the special revelation given to Paul, we now understand that we have redemption through Christ's precious blood, even the forgiveness of sins, when we believe the gospel. Christ is the fulfillment of the promise!

We must never underestimate the importance of *blood*, both as a biological mechanism in the human body and in our redemption. As King David pondered the wonderful workings of God in creation, he penned these words that echo down the halls of time to this very day: "I will praise thee; for I am fearfully and wonderfully made: marvelous are thy works; and that my soul knoweth right well" (Psa. 139:14). Robert J. Morgan makes the following observation of God's handiwork in regard to blood:

"Our bodies have a transportation system so complex and complete that it dwarfs that of a metropolis. The body's transportation system cuts through every tissue and organ by means of a network of sixty thousand miles of blood vessels. No cell of your body lies more than a hair's breadth from a blood capillary. The center of this vast system is a pump the size of an apple or a fist, that pumps two thousand gallons of blood through its chambers every day, sending blood to every part of the body. The blood carries vital, life-giving oxygen and nutrients to every cell in the body.

"The body has twenty-five trillion red blood cells, which are like little UPS trucks carrying all sorts of packages (such as oxygen) that are needed by the cells in the body. Every cell in the body requires oxygen to remain alive. If the blood is cut off to any part of the body, it deprives that part of the body of oxygen, and that bodily part will die. If the brain is deprived of oxygen, the brain dies, and the body dies.

"The white blood cells, meanwhile, are like billions of little tanks protecting the body. There are five different kinds of these white blood cells, and each one is trained to go after a different enemy. One drop of blood can contain anywhere from seven thousand to twenty-five thousand white blood cells, and the number of them increases when our body is fighting an illness, just like the government calling up the reserves.

"As far as our skeletal structure is concerned, our bones do double duty. Not only do they support the body, keep us upright, and keep us from being amoeba-like blobs, but they are hollow. On the inside of these bones are marvelous little factories that operate day and night, producing these billions of little trucks and tanks. The brain oversees the entire operation, and the heart keeps it functioning. Thirty-five hundred years ago, God told us, 'The life is in the blood.' And when Christ died, the life-giving blood drained from His body, providing forgiveness and life to all who believe."[3]

One of Satan's first major attempts to stamp out the bloodline of the Seed of the woman was to corrupt the human race in the days of Noah. While some believe the following passages refer to intermarriage between the godless line of

Cain and the godly line of Seth, we believe something far more sinister was taking place. If we stop and think about it, believers and unbelievers have been joined in marriage in every generation without the catastrophic results that we witness in the days of Noah.

> "And it came to pass...That the sons of God saw the daughters of men that they were fair; and they took them wives of all which they chose....There were giants in the earth in those days; and also after that, when the sons of God came in unto the daughters of men, and they bare children to them" (Gen. 6:1,2,4).

The title, "sons of God," is always a reference to angels in the Old Testament, never men, and in this specific instance, *fallen* angels (Job 1:6,7; 2:1). Apparently, Satan commissioned these fallen angels to leave their own habitation (heaven) for the unseemly purpose of corrupting the human race (Jude 6-8).

It appears that these evil creatures transformed themselves into a human form, which was well within their power. We know, for example, that the elect angels who visited Abraham and Lot appeared in a *physical* form. In fact, Abraham, and later, Lot washed their feet, and prepared a meal for them, "and they did eat" (Gen. 18; 19:1-11). It has also been suggested that the "sons of God" may have possessed men in the days of Noah, thus altering their metabolism. This was certainly true of Legion, who had superhuman strength (Mark 5:1-12).

Whatever the case might have been, we know the "sons of God" committed *fornication* with the daughters of men with catastrophic results. Dr. James M. Gray states that this sin would have been the confounding of two distinct orders of creatures and the production of a mixed race, partly human, partly superhuman, which would be just such a derangement of the divine plan as to warrant that which occurred, namely, the almost total extermination of all who were upon the earth.

This helps us to understand better the *severity* of the flood in the days of Noah. With the *exception* of Noah and his family, all flesh was destroyed from the face of the earth, which abruptly ended the corruption of the human race and the violence it perpetrated (Gen. 6:12,13). This also explains why *some* of the fallen host are already chained in the center of the earth, awaiting the judgment to come (II Pet. 2:4,5).

Having failed to corrupt Noah's family, Satan turned his attention to Israel after God raised up Abraham. The bloodline of the Seed of the woman was now reduced to one nation. Without a moment's hesitation, Satan focused his attention on destroying that nation. When Pharaoh decreed that all the male children in Israel were to be slain at birth, Satan was the one who was behind the evil plot. He knew that if he accomplished his purpose, the nation would be unable to propagate itself. But the midwives feared God and spared the little ones, thwarting the devil's scheme (Ex. 1:7-22).

Next, God reveals that the Redeemer would pass through the house of David; consequently, the seed of the woman is narrowed to one family (II Sam. 7:12-16; John 7:42). Satan wasted no time to set into motion his plan to destroy the seed of David. He used Athaliah, the wicked daughter of King Ahab and Jezebel to accomplish his end. After Athaliah's son Ahaziah was slain by Jehu, the Scriptures say "she arose and destroyed all the seed royal" (II Kings 11:1).

With the exception of little Joash, who was hidden in the storage room (bedchamber) by Jehosheba, Athaliah nearly accomplished her purpose. She had all the children of the royal seed murdered, or at least she thought she had. When

Athaliah ascended to the throne, she did not realize that Joash was alive and well. Joash was of the seed of David, which meant he was the rightful heir to the throne. The promise of God to bring a Redeemer into the world through David came down to one little boy.

The next chapter in the conflict of the ages took place in the days of King Herod. Satan himself was unaware when the Messiah would come into the world, so when he heard the wise men inquire of Herod, "Where is He that is born King of the Jews?" he was all ears (Matt. 2:2). Bethlehem!

Since Herod was consumed with staying in power, he customarily eliminated any threat to his throne, including having some of his own family members killed. With this in mind, Satan probably reminded Herod, "*You* are the king of the Jews!" If this was the case, it was an ingenious thing to point out to an egomaniac! This set into motion a tragic set of events known as the slaying of the innocents. All the children in Bethlehem and the surrounding region that were two years of age or under were slain. But unknown to Herod, God had already moved His Son out of the reach of his murderous exploits (Matt. 2:13-18). Satan came within a hair's breadth of thwarting the divine promise of a coming Redeemer, but once again, God, in His omniscience and sovereignty, out maneuvered His archenemy.

Although there would be other occasions during the life of Christ where Satan would try to destroy Him physically, the next chapter in the story brings us to Calvary. Having turned the tide of public opinion against Christ, the people cried out, "crucify Him, crucify Him" (Luke 23:21; John 19:6). Satan thought he had finally sealed His doom—he had finally destroyed the Seed of the woman! Little did he realize that Christ was securing redemption for all those who would place their faith in Him.

The Conflict of the Ages in the Tribulation

Christ crushed the head of the serpent at the Cross in fulfillment of Genesis 3:15, and completely defeated him. While Satan cannot undo Calvary—as much as he would like to (I Cor. 2:7,8)—the conflict of the ages continues in another way. Today Satan does everything in his power to keep men from coming to the truth of the gospel that Christ died for their sins and rose from the grave. He accomplishes his purpose by blinding men with religion and false doctrine. In the coming Day of the Lord, the conflict between good and evil, righteousness and unrighteousness, will intensify because the devil knows that his time is short.

> "And unto the angel of the church in Thyatira write; These things saith the Son of God, who hath His eyes like unto a flame of fire, and His feet are like fine brass" (Rev. 2:18).

> "But unto you I say, and unto the rest in Thyatira, as many as have not this doctrine, and which have not known the depths of Satan" (Rev. 2:24a).

Even though there is no question that the one addressing the seven churches in Asia is Christ, Thyatira is the first church where He is actually identified by name. The title "Son of God" has to do with the deity of Christ—Jesus Christ is God! He is the *eternal* Son of God. It has been correctly said that the Son of God became the Son of Man that the sons of men might become the sons of God.[4]

Notice, at this assembly, we have the teachings of the Son of God and the "depths of Satan" opposing the truth. This confirms that the conflict of the ages will continue through the Day of the Lord. In the age of grace, we are shown the deep things of God, but in the coming Tribulation, they will be exposed to the deep things of Satan (v. 24). Scary thought!

The titles *Son of God* and *Son of Man* combine to teach us that Christ is the perfect Judge. His eyes are said to be like a flame of fire that exposes the evil deeds of those who corrupt the Word of God at Thyatira. While the Lord is pleased with the love and patience of this assembly and commends them for these virtues, there are those in their midst who *tolerate* Jezebel and her evil teachings.

> "Notwithstanding I have a few things against thee, because thou sufferest that woman Jezebel, which calleth herself a prophetess, to teach and to seduce my servants to commit fornication, and to eat things sacrificed unto idols" (Rev. 2:20).

Although it is doubtful that this prophetess's name will actually be Jezebel, the Lord assigns this designation to her simply because her evil exploits mirror those of the Jezebel in the Old Testament. Jezebel of old was the epitome of evil! Perhaps we should pause here a moment to consider her background and evil ways, which will help us better understand her namesake at Thyatira.

Jezebel was the daughter of Ethbaal, king of the Zidonians, whom we would know to be the Phoenicians. Notice that her father's name, *Ethbaal*, has attached to it the name of the pagan God, Baal. He was a Baal worshipper, and the same can be said of his daughter, Jezebel. They were both idol worshippers! When Ahab, the king of northern Israel, married Jezebel, he forged an alliance with the Phoenicians to help secure his borders, but he got more than he bargained for in the relationship.

Jezebel was as wicked as they come. She was domineering, merciless, and cold as ice. Ahab did evil in the sight of the Lord when he married the *unbelieving* Jezebel who deliberately drew him away from Jehovah. It is said of him that he "went and served Baal, and worshipped him" (I Kings

16:30,31). After he erected an altar and a grove to Baal on her behalf, Jezebel introduced *witchcraft* and *whoredom* (fornication) into Israel's worship of Baal (I Kings 16:32,33 cf. II Kings 9:22).

Jezebel hated, with a passion, the prophets of God and killed the ones she could find, but the queen relished the company of the prophets of Baal and had them dine with her at the queen's table (I Kings 18:13,19). And you can be sure that some of the dishes on the menu would have included things that had previously been sacrificed to idols. When Ahab told Jezebel that Elijah had called fire down from heaven consuming the altar and slaying her prophets, she sent this message to Elijah: "So let the gods do to me, and more also, if I make not thy life as the life of one of them by tomorrow about this time" (I Kings 19:1,2). The threats of this woman could make the hair on the back of your neck stand up! Elijah knew this wasn't an idle threat, and took the first chariot out of town!

On another occasion, after Naboth refused to sell his vineyard to Ahab, the king was sorrowful and pouted. In short, he was depressed. Jezebel wasn't about to take this lying down; she *framed* Naboth and had him stoned to death so her husband could take possession of the vineyard (I Kings 21:5-16). This devilish act resulted in Jezebel being cast out a window and eaten of dogs, as foretold by Elijah (I Kings 21:17-23 cf. II Kings 9:30-37).

> "Notwithstanding I have a few things against thee, because thou sufferest that woman Jezebel, which calleth herself a prophetess, to teach and to seduce my servants to commit fornication, and to eat things sacrificed unto idols" (Rev. 2:20).

As Jezebel of old led Israel away to commit fornication with the temple prostitutes, the Jezebel at Thyatira will seduce the servants of the Lord to commit *spiritual* fornication. As a prophetess, who supposedly ministers in spiritual things, she will probably claim to have received a special revelation from God that His servants should pledge their allegiance to the one-world church to have a greater outreach. Those who fail to do so will be unmercifully persecuted. The one-world church is an amalgamation of religions that, in the course of the Tribulation, will make up the *religious* arm of the Antichrist's kingdom. Essentially, it will be a state church similar to ancient Babylon that operated under the auspices of "unity," apart from God (Gen. 11 cf. Rev. 17 & 18).

> "And I gave her space to repent of her fornication; and she repented not. Behold, I will cast her into a bed, and them that commit adultery with her into great tribulation, except they repent of their deeds" (Rev. 2:21,22).

We learn from this passage that God calls upon her to repent of her evil deeds; He does so through the ministry of His chosen apostles and prophets at that time (Rev. 18:20). But when Jezebel refuses to repent, she is warned that if she continues in her rebellion, she will be cast down like Jezebel of old, but in this case "into a bed," along with those who commit adultery with her. In other words, the Lord is going to cast her into the Great Tribulation where she and her followers will suffer a death similar to the horrible fate of Jezebel in the Old Testament and the prophets of Baal who were slain by the edge of the sword.

> "And all the churches shall know that I am He which searcheth the reins and hearts: and I will give unto every one of you according to your works. But unto you I say, and unto the rest in Thyatira, as many as have not this doctrine, and which have not known the depths of Satan, as they speak; I will put upon you none other burden" (Rev. 2:23,24).

The eyes of the Son of God pierce straight through the "reins and hearts" of men, exposing their wicked ways. There is nothing in the secret chambers of the innermost being that is hidden from His penetrating gaze. With "His feet like fine brass," which depicts judgment, He will judge these evildoers according to their works. As the Scriptures say, "Vengeance is mine; I will repay, saith the Lord" (Rom. 12:19). Interestingly, the ungodly teachings of Jezebel will reach far beyond the church of Thyatira to the other churches in Asia as well. So wisdom says that the warning here is to all these assemblies. Thank God that there will be a remnant in this church that will not be taken in by Jezebel's false doctrine and influence and will therefore, not know the depths of Satan.

> "And he that overcometh, and keepeth my works unto the end, to him will I give power over the nations: And he shall rule them with a rod of iron; as the vessels of a potter shall they be broken to shivers: even as I received of my Father. And I will give him the morning star" (Rev. 2:26-28).

This particular promise to the overcomers who endure to the end of the Tribulation is rooted in Psalms 2:8,9. This prophecy in Psalms regarding ruling over the nations and judging them was originally given to the Son by the heavenly Father. But this passage in Revelation is a clear indication that the promise of ruling over the nations is to be shared with those who do not give themselves over to the depths of Satan in the Tribulation. The fulfillment of this will be when the "morning star," who is Christ, returns to establish His Kingdom on the earth (Rev. 22:16).

The practical lesson we glean from this assembly is the importance of *separation*. If you read the context of this letter carefully, while some at Thyatira were completely deceived by Jezebel, others within the assembly knew what she was teaching was wrong, but tolerated it. May it never be said of us that we went along with something we knew was not right merely to keep peace and avoid criticism. "It is a grave mistake to underestimate sin and strive for no-fault moralities."[5]

5

The Kingdom Church at Sardis and Philadelphia (Part 1)

"What thou seest, write in a book, and send it unto the seven churches which are in Asia; unto Ephesus, and unto Smyrna, and unto Pergamos, and unto Thyatira, and unto Sardis, and unto Philadelphia, and unto Laodicea."

—Revelation 1:11

THE JEWISH ASSEMBLY AT SARDIS

The following story of a man who was in charge of a drawbridge is a good example of how one decision can alter your life. It is a solemn reminder that the influence of others can cloud your judgment to do that which is right.

"As a boat came up the river, the people on the boat asked the keeper to lift the bridge so they could pass. 'No,' said the keeper, 'it will soon be time for the train and I might not get it back down.' But the captain of the boat convinced him that it would take only a very few minutes and that he had plenty of time. Against his better judgment, he lifted the bridge, but before it had been let down, the passenger train, going about sixty miles an hour, came thundering around the curve. In spite of all that could be done, it plunged through the open bridge into the river. When the keeper saw the tragic scene and heard the cries of the injured, his reason became unbalanced and he was taken to an asylum, where he was heard to cry: 'O if I only had not!' All through the dark hours of the night he could be heard,

'O if I only had not.' We wonder if the lost in Hell will be heard crying, 'O if I only had not trifled with God.'"[1]

> "And unto the angel of the church in Sardis write; These things saith He that hath the seven Spirits of God, and the seven stars; I know thy works, that thou hast a name that thou livest, and art dead" (Rev. 3:1).

The church at Sardis will find itself under the spell of the world in the coming Day of the Lord. Like the drawbridge operator, unless they repent, they will be drawn into a state of complacency that will lead them down a path from which there is no return. They will trifle with God with catastrophic results. Up to this point, the Lord has *commended* these Kingdom assemblies in one way or another, but such is not the case with the local assembly at Sardis. Sadly, there is no word of commendation to this church. Instead they are sternly rebuked and warned of the eternal consequences of their unbelief.

As John addresses the minister of the assembly at Sardis, he begins by identifying the source of this special revelation. There's little question that this message is from the Son of Man, Who is said to have the seven spirits of God before Him, and the seven stars in His right hand.

Although it is generally believed that the *seven spirits of God* are seven attributes of the Holy Spirit, we respectfully disagree. As we noted in an earlier chapter, the Holy Spirit is coequal and coeternal with the Father and the Son. He is God! (See Acts 5:3,4.) Seeing that these seven spirits stand *before* the throne in a position of subordination, we can safely conclude that the Holy Spirit is not in view (Rev. 1:4 cf. 4:5). He is equal with God, not subordinate to Him. Furthermore, we're to understand that Christ is in *possession* of these seven spirit beings, who are subject to His control, according to our passage under consideration.

These seven spirits of God are seven angelic beings of the highest heavenly order. They stand before God day and night, prepared to execute His every command. Each of the seven churches in Asia has assigned to it, as a witness, one of these seven angels. When Christ confesses the names of those who are faithful before His Father at the judgment to come, this particular group of angels will be present. They will also bear witness against those who deny the Son of Man in these churches (Luke 12:8,9 cf. Rev. 3:5). The "seven stars" are the seven ministers of these Jewish assemblies. They, too, will be present at the judgment, as His *possession*, to bear witness for or against those entrusted to their spiritual oversight (Heb. 13:17).

The Lord exposes this church for what it is—a lie! He states, "I know thy works, that thou hast a name that thou livest, and art dead." This will be a very religious assembly. In the eyes of the world, this church will be alive, vibrant, and contemporary. Sardis will be the place to worship! It will probably be difficult to find a seat when they gather on the Sabbath. The "works" spoken of here are in relation to making a *name* for themselves.

Mark these words and mark them well: When the world sings the praises of a church, you can be relatively sure it's dead spiritually. Sardis will have the *form* of godliness, but in reality, they will deny the Lord who bought them (II Pet. 2:1,2). If a church is small and seemingly insignificant, the world will pronounce it dead, when the reverse is normally true. It is these types of assemblies that are usually *rich* spiritually because they faithfully obey the Savior, such as we saw at Smyrna. While the church at Sardis will have the outward appearance of life, the Lord peered into the heart of this assembly and pronounced it spiritually dead. This doesn't mean there won't be a remnant in this assembly that knows and loves the Lord; rather, the Lord is speaking about the general state of this church. Those who attend this gathering in that day will hear everything known to man except the truth of the gospel!

WATCHING AND WAITING

"Be watchful, and strengthen the things which remain, that are ready to die: for I have not found thy works perfect before God. Remember therefore how thou hast received and heard, and hold fast, and repent. If therefore thou shalt not watch, I will come on thee as a thief, and thou shalt not know what hour I will come upon thee" (Rev. 3:2,3).

We must constantly keep before us that John is addressing Israel *nationally.* As we know, the chosen nation in time past was made up of both believers and unbelievers; the same will be true in the future, as these passages plainly indicate. The Lord particularly appeals to the Israelites in this assembly who had not yet fully come under the spell of liberalism and worldliness.

It is essential to remember John had been transported into the future Tribulation when he wrote these words (Rev. 1:9,10). This raises the question, what had this assembly "received and heard"? Because the coming Day of the Lord is inseparably bound to the prophetic program and the Kingdom, there is no question that the *Kingdom gospel* had been preached to them (Matt. 24:14). They had "heard" it from the future Kingdom apostles and prophets (Rev. 18:20) who had "received" it from the Lord. Those who had initially heard the gospel at Sardis but rejected it were to "hold fast" to it and "repent." They are to do works of repentance, which will include being water baptized. In so doing, they will restore their covenant relationship with God, paving the way for them to acknowledge that Jesus is their Messiah (John 1:31 cf. 20:31).

A short time ago I was sitting at a major intersection waiting for the stoplight to change. As I was watching the cross-traffic that was traveling at a high rate of speed, a lady pulled into the center of the intersection to make a left turn. She obviously wasn't paying attention, due to the fact that she was talking on a cell phone. The next thing I know, she hit the accelerator, cutting across two lanes of oncoming traffic. Cars were flying off the road in every direction to avoid hitting her. One driver missed her by half of a gnat's eyelash—and that's close!

The first thought that crossed my mind was, a guy could get killed out here! At the speeds those cars were traveling, if one of them would have hit her, someone would have probably been killed. The next thing that came to mind was that we are only one heartbeat away from eternity. Are you ready? If Christ were to return for His Church today in what is commonly known as the Rapture, can you confidently say you would spend eternity with Him?

The same question is posed to the church at Sardis in regard to the *Second Coming of Christ* to the earth. Will they be watching and waiting for the Lord's return to deliver them from the Antichrist and usher them into the blessings of the Kingdom? This question was originally raised by our Lord, during His earthly ministry to Israel, in the parable of the *Ten Virgins*. If you compare this parable with the revelation John delivered to the church at Sardis, there are striking similarities. In fact, we might say this particular parable is a mini-commentary on Revelation 3.

The Setting of the Story

"Then shall the kingdom of heaven be likened unto ten virgins, which took their lamps, and went forth to meet the bridegroom. And five of them were wise, and five were foolish" (Matt. 25:1,2).

When we study Matthew, Mark, Luke, and John, we are not studying four different gospels. We are studying one gospel, the *gospel of the Kingdom*, from four different vantage points. Matthew, Mark, Luke, and John are merely an extension of the Law and the Prophets.

We must remember, then, that when our Lord spoke the parable of the *Ten Virgins* to His disciples, the Mystery was still a secret hidden in the mind of God. Therefore, the coming of Christ spoken of in this parable is not the *Secret Coming of Christ* for His Church, called the Rapture, that we referred to a moment ago. Rather, the *Second Coming of Christ* is in view. This parable must be interpreted in relation to the prophetic program in which it is found.

It is very important to distinguish between a fable and a parable. A fable is a fictitious story of supernatural happenings. Usually animals or insects talk to one another and act like humans. The story is not true and could never be true, but it does teach a moral or a lesson. In contrast, a *parable* is taken from a real life experience. It is true story or it could be a true story. Many of our Lord's parables were based on fact, such as the story of the Prodigal son— *"A certain man had two sons."* When the Lord taught the parable of the wheat and tares, He could well have been in view of a field. But even if He was somewhere else, such as the upper room, when He spoke it, it was still true or could be true.

A parable always implies an analogy. It is something that is placed alongside to illustrate a truth. So then, the parable before us is true; it actually happened in the Lord's time or it could have happened. The ten virgins represent something and the bridegroom speaks of someone. It is not necessary to interpret every detail of a parable. There is usually one primary theme the Lord would have us see. In this case, it is to be *prepared, ready,* and *watchful* for His return (vv. 10-13).

The Narrative

In the foregoing passage, "the kingdom of heaven" is a reference to the Millennial Kingdom. There is both a spiritual and physical aspect to it. In this context, we do well to remember that this is not a kingdom in Heaven, but one that originates from Heaven. This phrase is only used by Matthew because he consistently traces the kingship of Christ. Consequently, the Kingdom that will one day be established upon the earth is going to be a rule of God—the theocracy will again be restored.

The number 10 in the Bible signifies "the perfection of divine order."[2] It carries the idea of *completeness* of order. For example:

The Ten Commandments contain all the moral law of God.

The tithe, a *tenth* part, was what was due from man to God.

The ten virgins represent the nation Israel in her entirety. Complete!

Matthew 25 deals with three areas of the Kingdom to come: *profession* (vv. 1-13); *service* (vv. 14-30); and the *testing of the Gentiles* (vv. 31-46).

The Ten Virgins

The first part of the narrative is not dealing with service, but Israel's relationship to Christ. The five wise virgins represent believing Israel, those who have placed their faith in the Messiah and did the required works of repentance. They had a *proper attitude* toward Him! The foolish virgins represent those Israelites who gave the Bridegroom lip service, but their heart was far from Him. They were only interested in *personal gain.*

An example of the wise and foolish virgins would be the twelve apostles of the Kingdom. Eleven of the apostles had placed their faith in Messiah and gladly performed the necessary works of repentance (Luke 3:8). Judas likewise did these works. He was water baptized, performed miracles, and served as the treasurer of the group (Matt. 10:5-8; John 12:4-6). In fact, the other apostles believed he was one of them in the faith. It shows us how far the religious unsaved will go to be accepted among true believers. They often deceive themselves into thinking they are right with God, as we see at Sardis. But the Lord exposed Judas for who he was—an *unbeliever!* (John 6:68-71). You see, Judas was only interested in how the Kingdom could benefit him. He was extremely selfish!

Lamps, Oil, and the Word of God

"They that were foolish took their lamps, and took no oil with them: But the wise took oil in their vessels with their lamps. While the bridegroom tarried, they all slumbered and slept" (Matt. 25:3-5).

The lamps here are unquestionably a reference to the Word of God (Psa. 119:105). Solomon says in Proverbs 6:23, "The law is light." The oil represents the Holy Spirit who moved holy men of God to bring us the inspired Word of God (II Pet. 1:21). Of course, it is the Holy Spirit who illuminates the believer to the truth of God's Word.

The *wise* virgins had stored the Word of God in their hearts; they were prepared and watching for the Lord's return. But the *foolish* virgins, while under the *sound* of the Word, had not received it, nor had they stored it in their hearts. They were negligent! They heard the truth, but had not received it to be saved.

"And at midnight there was a cry made, Behold, the bridegroom cometh; go ye out to meet him. Then all those virgins arose, and trimmed their lamps. And the foolish said unto the wise, Give us of your oil; for our lamps are gone out. But the wise answered, saying, Not so; lest there be not enough for us and you: but go ye rather to them that sell, and buy for yourselves" (Matt. 25:6-9).

When the announcement was made that the bridegroom was coming, the five foolish virgins were left standing in the dark. They are instructed by the others to find those that sell the light-giving oil and buy it for themselves. The Scriptures instruct us to **"Buy the truth, and sell it not**; also wisdom, and instruction, and understanding" (Prov. 23:23). Who were the sellers of truth? Who could provide this commodity? Simple, it was those who minister the Word— pastors, teachers, and rabbis. But it's too late! It's night; they are nowhere to be found. You see, the true ministers of the Word will also go out to meet the Bridegroom.

"And while they went to buy, the Bridegroom came; and they that were ready went in with Him to the marriage: and the door was shut. Afterward came also the other virgins, saying, Lord, Lord, open to us. But He answered and said, Verily I say unto you, I know you not" (Matt. 25:10-12).

When the five foolish virgins went to find the truth as to how to be saved, the Bridegroom came. Christ is the Bridegroom! When He returns He will receive His own to Himself and the door will be shut. It will be shut and stay shut! When the five foolish virgins request to come in they are refused entrance. The Lord will say to them, "I know you not." (See also Matt. 7:21-23.)

"Watch therefore, for ye know neither the day nor the hour wherein the Son of Man cometh" (Matt. 25:13).

This is a clear reference to the Second Coming of Christ, when the Lord will return as a thief in the night (I Thes. 5:2;

II Pet. 3:10). When we apply this parable to the church at Sardis, interestingly, the Lord warns the assembly to *watch*. Be prepared, be ready, don't be caught off guard like the five foolish virgins who neglected the salvation of God.

Another reason that we are not the subject of these seven letters has to do with the *hope* of these Kingdom believers. If John was writing to the members of the Body of Christ, as many teach, then the Rapture would have to be post-Tribulational because the hope he holds out to his readers is the *Second Coming of Christ*. For those who rightly divide the Word of truth, this is unthinkable!

> "If therefore thou shalt not watch, I will come on thee as a thief, and thou shalt not know what hour I will come upon thee. Thou hast a few names even in Sardis which have not defiled their garments" (Rev. 3:3b,4a).

Like the five wise virgins in the parable, there will be "a few names" at Sardis who will not go along with the worldly ways of this assembly to make a name for themselves. It is sad, though, that the foolish in the assembly will do so and will be in danger of being blotted out of the Book of Life. This is why there is a sense of urgency to call them to repentance before it's too late.

> "He that overcometh, the same shall be clothed in white raiment; and I will not blot out his name out of the Book of Life, but I will confess his name before my Father, and before His angels" (Rev. 3:5).

Once again, similar to the five wise virgins, the overcomers at Sardis will not have their names blotted out of the Book of Life.[3] They will be clothed in white garments and granted entrance into the Kingdom. Their garments will be made white by the blood of the Lamb. In other words, they will be clothed in the righteousness of God. Practically speaking, this will be the physical manifestation of the righteousness of the saints, which speaks of their faithful service that will be acknowledged by Christ before the Father and His holy angels (Rev. 7:14 cf. 19:8).

THE JEWISH ASSEMBLY AT PHILADELPHIA

"And to the angel of the church in Philadelphia write; These things saith He that is holy, He that is true, He that hath the key of David, He that openeth, and no man shutteth; and shutteth, and no man openeth" (Rev. 3:7).

If there has been any question as to whether or not the Apostle John has been addressing Jewish kingdom assemblies, all doubt is completely dispelled in the letter to the church at Philadelphia. Both the terminology and phraseology of this communication are deeply rooted in the prophetic program. For example, in these first seven verses of Chapter 3, John makes reference to "the key of David," "the synagogue," "the hour of temptation" (Great Tribulation), "the temple of my God," "the city of my God, which is the New Jerusalem," etc.

The coming Tribulation will be characterized by unholy acts and lies, which stand in stark contrast to Christ who is *holy* and *true*, as noted by the apostle in his introduction. The attribute of holiness has to do with Christ's moral perfection; He always does what is *right*. It is the one attribute that encompasses all others. For instance, because Christ is holy, He always speaks the truth. While every believer rests in this fact, this will be particularly reassuring to the Tribulation saints who will live in a day of pervasive deception. They will be able to trust what Christ says, based on the knowledge that God cannot lie! (Titus 1:2).

John's reference to "the key of David" harkens back to the days of King Hezekiah. Due to the arrogance of Shebna, the treasurer and principal officer of Hezekiah's court, God stripped Shebna of his position and sent him into exile. In his place, He appointed Eliakim. It is wondrous that, according to Gardner, Eliakim means, "God raises up,"[4] of whom the following is said:

> "And it shall come to pass in that day, that I will call my servant Eliakim the son of Hilkiah: And I will clothe him with thy [Shebna's] robe, and strengthen him [Eliakim] with thy girdle, and I will commit thy government into his hand: and he shall be a father to the inhabitants of Jerusalem, and to the house of Judah. And the key of the house of David will I lay upon his [Eliakim's] shoulder; so he shall open, and none shall shut; and he shall shut, and none shall open" (Isa. 22:20-22).

As is the case with many Old Testament prophecies, there is a short-term fulfillment and oftentimes a long-range fulfillment, which is certainly true in this case. Notice, the "government" and "the key of the house of David" were given to Eliakim. Clearly Eliakim was a type of Christ. Christ, then, is a fulfillment of this prophecy because we know the government will be placed upon His shoulder in the Millennial Kingdom (Isa. 9:6; Jer. 23:5). Additionally, the Lord reveals to the church at Philadelphia that He possesses the key of David (Rev. 3:7); He is the rightful heir to the throne of David; He alone is the supreme authority, as the key of David implies.

The same spirit of arrogance that compelled Shebna to rebel against God will also consume the Antichrist. He, like Shebna, will be sent into exile (in the Lake of Fire) when the Lord returns to overthrow Antichrist's kingdom and establish His own kingdom of righteousness.

But what is the significance that the one who possesses this key has the authority to "openeth, and no man shutteth;

and shutteth, and no man openeth"? Normally this is taken to mean that the Lord will open and close doors of opportunity to serve Him in the Tribulation. Although God does sometimes operate this way in other portions of the Scripture, it cannot be the case in this context. Instead, we are to understand that the Lord has the power to open and close doors of *deliverance*, as we are going to see.

> "I know thy works: behold, I have set before thee an open door, and no man can shut it: for thou hast a little strength, and hast kept My Word, and hast not denied My name" (Rev. 3:8).

A Poignant Love Story

In his book, *Many a Tear Has to Fall*, Wayne Hudson tells a touching story about a farmer who lived in Kansas.

"It was 1898 and Ben had left the east 8 years ago to head out west in hopes of making his fortune. Well he wasn't rich, but he had accumulated over 300 acres of good land and built a comfortable farm house on it. He raised wheat, corn, and all of his vegetables. He had managed to build his herd of cattle to over 200 head. Having accomplished all of this in only 8 years, he decided that it was now time.

"The ad that he placed in the New York newspaper said, 'Wanted: A good woman willing to be a pen pal. Marriage is a possibility for the right woman.' Before long, he began receiving letters from Molly. Their correspondence soon turned into love for each other. Now, here he stood in the Kansas City train station waiting to finally meet her.

"When the train arrived, there were a lot of women getting off. Suddenly, he yelled, 'Molly—over here!'

"She looked his way, walked over to him, smiled and held out her hand. He took it for a moment, and then let it go. She said, 'How did you know who I was?'

"He then reached into the back pocket of his overalls and said, 'From these here letters.'

"'But there are no pictures in them.'

"He dropped his head a bit and said, 'Oh yes there are! There are lots of pictures in your words.'

"You see, he had spent hours reading every word—looking for every little clue that would tell him who Molly really was. He had fallen in love with her words—words that had painted her portrait.

"God's precious Word paints a vivid portrait of who He is. We...should fall in love with His Word so that we can then fall in love with its Author."[5]

Since the beginning of time, the Word of God has been under attack (Gen. 3:1-5) and things haven't changed much down through the centuries. Today, when spiritual leaders say, "Let's not emphasize the blood of Christ; it's too repulsive; someone might be offended," this is a direct *assault* on the Scriptures (Gal. 5:11). Those who say, "We've had enough doctrine, we only want to hear about Christian living," are *ignoring* the Word of God (Titus 1:9; 2:1). When men challenge the preaching of Jesus Christ according to the revelation of the Mystery, they are *denying* a clear command of God's Word (Rom. 16:25; Eph. 3:8,9).

These are all serious departures from the faith, but they pale by comparison with what lies ahead in the future Tribulation, when Satan will attempt to completely corrupt the Word of God, and kill those who preserve, defend, and proclaim it (Rev. 6:9; 13:4-7; 22:18,19). In spite of the consequences, the believers at Philadelphia will *keep* His Word and not deny His name, for which they are commended by the Lord. Like the farmer who loved to read the words of his fiancée, these saints will fall in love with the words of their first love. They will store them in their hearts that they might not sin against Him (Psa. 119:9-11).

> "Behold, I will make them of the synagogue of Satan, which say they are Jews, and are not, but do lie; behold, I will make them to come and worship before thy feet, and to know that I have loved thee" (Rev. 3:9).

Our Lord was confronted with the same problem when He entered the synagogue at Nazareth. When He shared the truth with them, they were filled with animosity and took Him outside the city and tried to throw Him off a cliff (Luke 4:28-30). In similar fashion, because these Kingdom saints at Philadelphia uphold the truth and refuse to deny Christ is the Messiah of Israel, they will be denied access to the synagogue to worship. They will be ostracized by their own countrymen. But the Lord exposes these Jews of the synagogue of Satan as those who are living a *lie*.

At the judgment of Israel and the nations, these very Jews who persecuted the believers at Philadelphia will fall at *their* feet, as they bow to worship the Messiah they blatantly rejected. At that day, they will give an account of their sinful actions and will be made to acknowledge the Lord's love for these Philadelphian saints (Matt. 24:45-51 cf. 25:24-36).

6

The Kingdom Church at Philadelphia (Part 2) and Laodicea

"Because thou hast kept the Word of my patience, I also will keep thee from the hour of temptation, which shall come upon all the world, to try them that dwell upon the earth. Behold, I come quickly: hold that fast which thou hast, that no man take thy crown."

—*Revelation 3:10,11*

THE HOUR OF TEMPTATION

Most dispensationalists stand united that the *hour of temptation* or trial spoken of here by the Lord is a clear reference to the latter part of the Tribulation period known as the Great Tribulation. We, of course, would concur! The problem is, since most Acts 2 dispensationalists believe John is addressing the Church, the Body of Christ, they conclude the Lord is speaking about the catching away of the Church sometime before the Great Tribulation. This is nothing short of a failure to rightly divide the Word of truth and leaves the door wide open for a mid-tribulational Rapture.

Whether you believe John was writing to believers in his day or in the future, as we hold, in either case he is addressing the *Kingdom church*, not the Church, the Body of Christ. Therefore, the passage before us must be interpreted in relation to the earthly ministry of Christ to Israel. If you remove Paul's epistles from your thinking for a moment, you will find that the four Gospels and the Book of Revelation dovetail together perfectly. This is because they are both dealing with the same subject matter: Christ and the Kingdom to come!

It is very important to read closely the Lord's words to this assembly: "I also will keep thee from the hour of temptation." Notice that the promise to the saints at Philadelphia is not to sustain them through the Great Tribulation, but to *keep them from it.* Unlike the other assemblies in Asia, the church at Philadelphia will not enter into unholy alliances or compromise the faith. This assembly is commended for keeping the Word of His patience in the face of death; thus, they are promised *deliverance* from the last three and one-half years of the Tribulation.

In the body of this letter, we learn that the Lord has the key of David and the authority to open a door of deliverance and the power to close it. We are then told the believers at Philadelphia will have set before them "an open door, and no man can shut it." This is followed by the promise that the Lord would keep or deliver them "from the hour of temptation." We can confidently say *deliverance* is the theme of this letter.

While this promise is primarily intended for the believers at Philadelphia, it will undoubtedly be extended to all those in that day who, like the Philadelphians, keep the Word of God and refuse to deny His name. This is the faithful remnant that will gradually emerge out of the early years of the Tribulation. They are the ones who will be promised deliverance from the Great Tribulation.

The Lord says of this period that it will "come upon all the world, to try them that dwell upon the earth" (Rev. 3:10). This statement finds its origin in the Olivet Discourse, where we read, "For then shall be great tribulation, such as was not since the beginning of the world to this time, no, nor ever shall be" (Matt. 24:21). Although the wrath of

God is clearly witnessed in the early part of the Tribulation, it is greatly intensified in the latter half, as God prepares to overthrow the kingdoms of this evil world system and establish the Kingdom of His dear Son (Rev. 11:15).

When the inhabitants of the earth pass from the Tribulation to the Great Tribulation, they will witness a series of judgments that will buckle the knees of a strong man and cause kings to weep and mourn. Entire cities, including Babylon, will be leveled under the weight of these judgments. Evil will sweep over the world like an eerie fog as Satan and his wicked hosts roam the earth. Then it will all draw to a climax at Armageddon, where there will be a bloodbath of biblical proportions. It is from these catastrophic events that the faithful remnant is promised deliverance.

> "Behold, I come quickly: hold that fast which thou hast, that no man take thy crown" (Rev. 3:11).

But is this deliverance out of harm's way confirmed by other Scriptures? On this point, we will allow the Scriptures to speak for themselves. As we will learn when we study Revelation Chapter 12, the "man child" of Isaiah 66:7-8 and Revelation 12:1-6 are one and the same. Throughout the prophetic Scriptures, it is plainly stated that Israel will one day *return* to the Lord, which will result in her ultimate *restoration* in the Kingdom to come. The first indication of this approaching day is the birth of the man child in the middle of the Tribulation. We believe this is a reference to a special group of Jewish believers who totally devote themselves to the Lord during the first three and one-half years of Jacob's Trouble. They are the faithful remnant gathered out from the seven churches in Asia, as we have been careful to acknowledge in our exegesis of the church at Philadelphia.

In essence, Isaiah says that, *before* Israel enters the Great Tribulation, she brings forth; that is, *before* her labor pains begin due to intense persecution, she will deliver a child. Prior to her final restoration, there will be a *premature* birth in Israel—a male child. The child, then, is representative of those believers who will "overcome" the evil one, as a result of their complete obedience to God. Subsequently, they are promised deliverance *from* the Great Tribulation. What is true of this faithful remnant is also true of the "man child" (Rev. 2:26,27 cf. 12:5).

This event is a *foretaste* of Israel's future *restoration*, similar to the resurrection of the saints who arose after the resurrection of Christ. These saints who arose and went into Jerusalem (Matt. 27:52,53) were a *token* of what was yet to come in the first resurrection at the Second Coming of Christ.

Like Elijah, who was caught up into heaven in a whirlwind without ever experiencing death, the same will be true of this faithful remnant. We should pause here to make it perfectly clear that the removal of these faithful Israelites must **not** be confused with the translation of the Church, which is His Body. The Rapture of the Church will have already taken place years earlier.

After the faithful remnant is removed from the earth, Israel (the woman) will be ushered into the wilderness where Satan will attempt to destroy her. But God will intervene on her behalf and assist her through the remainder of the Great Tribulation (Rev. 12:13-16), as He did in time past when He protected His people in Goshen (Ex. 8:22; 9:26).

THE REWARD OF THE INHERITANCE

"Him that overcometh will I make a pillar in the temple of my God, and he shall go no more out: and I will write upon him the name of my God, and the name of the city of my God, which is new Jerusalem, which cometh down out of heaven from my God: and I will write upon him my new name" (Rev. 3:12).

These promises to the Kingdom saints are so far removed from the Body of Christ that it is inconceivable how anyone could miss the contrast, but some do. The members of the Body of Christ are not promised to be pillars in the temple of God; *we are* the temple of God in the administration of Grace (Eph. 2:21).

The imagery of pillars is introduced early in the history of Israel, so the people of Israel were very familiar with the concept and purpose of the pillar. When Solomon had his temple built in Jerusalem, the master craftsmen erected two magnificent pillars at the entrance of the house of God. The one on the right was called Jachin, which means, "He will establish," and the one on the left was named Boaz, meaning, "Strength is in Him" (II Chron. 3:15-17). This certainly could be said of the church at Philadelphia, who found their strength in Christ; He alone had established them in the truth of the Kingdom gospel. But we believe the promise here has a far greater significance.

The promise to the saints at Philadelphia is to be a pillar in the temple, which, of course, is a figure of speech in this context. Like the pillars of the *Parthenon* at Athens, they will still be standing when everything else lies in ruins. Since the temple in the New Jerusalem is Almighty God and the Lamb (Rev. 21:22), those who overcome the evil one and refuse the mark of the beast will be the eternal pillars of it. That they will "go no more out" means that they will never again be exposed to the trials and temptations of this evil world system, but will dwell in His righteous, eternal presence throughout eternity.

As they are welcomed into the New Jerusalem, they will step into the eternal state on the new earth. While they are taking in the wonders of their new surroundings, Christ will bestow upon them the distinct honor of writing upon them "the name of my God, and the name of the city of my God, which is new Jerusalem, which cometh down out of heaven from my God: and I will write upon him my new name." There won't be any problem identifying these dear brethren.

A PRACTICAL NOTE

We are indeed thankful that we will never face what these saints will encounter in the future, but this does not mean believers today are exempt from having problems. The important thing is to be prepared in advance for them. The believers at Philadelphia didn't simply read the Scriptures devotionally; they were well-grounded in the Word. They *kept* the Word of God. In order to "keep the Word," you must first know it, which will enable you to make an application of it when you find yourself faced with a problem.

You will notice that, when you are experiencing a crisis in your life, everyone has a word of advice for you. Job encountered the same thing. But the advice he received from Eliphaz, Bildad, and Zophar wasn't sound counsel and only served to complicate Job's suffering. If you are going through a difficult time, the first one you should consult is your pastor. He should be able to give you the assistance you need in the Word to resolve the issue. If your pastor is unable to help, he should know a godly *Christian* counselor who will be in a position to get to the bottom of the matter. But here's the *key*: you will need to submit yourself to the counsel of the Word of God, even though it may not be what you want to hear.

The more time we spend with the Word of God, the more we will find ourselves falling in love with His words. This

will result in a deeper relationship and a closer walk with
its Author.

THE JEWISH ASSEMBLY AT LAODICEA

"And unto the angel of the church of the Laodiceans
write; These things saith the Amen, the faithful and
true Witness, the Beginning of the creation of God"
(Rev. 3:14).

The last of the seven churches in Asia is Laodicea. This
church should not be confused with the assembly of the
same name in the Apostle Paul's writings. The saints Paul
addressed at Laodicea were members of the Body of Christ
who were saved under the gospel of the grace of God. In his
epistle to the Colossians, the apostle states:

"For I would that ye knew what great conflict I have
for you, and for them at Laodicea, and for as many as
have not seen my face in the flesh; That their hearts
might be comforted, being knit together in love, and
unto all riches of the full assurance of understanding,
to the acknowledgement of the mystery of God" (Col.
2:1,2).

Although Paul had never personally seen these saints, he
had a great burden for them, that they might have a "full
assurance of understanding." But the only way for them to
have this assurance was to acknowledge the Mystery. Paul
instructs them that the Colossian letter should be read in
the church of the Laodiceans, and the letter from Laodicea,
probably Ephesians, should be read by the Colossians (Col.
4:16). The point is this: both Ephesians and Colossians are
written exclusively to the Body of Christ.

So then, the assembly Paul addressed at Laodicea was
comprised of Gentile believers who understood the revelation of the Mystery. In contrast, the Apostle John is

instructed to write to the church of the Laodiceans in the future Day of the Lord. This is a *Jewish assembly* that will be under the sound of the Kingdom gospel, as John clearly points out in the letter.

> "These things saith the Amen, the faithful and true Witness, the Beginning of the creation of God" (Rev. 3:14).

The purpose of a title is to give a general description of a person or work. For example, the book title, *One Minute After You Die*, gives you a pretty good idea that the subject of the book is life after death. This same principle is true of our Lord, Who possesses numerous titles and names, one of which is "the Amen." He is called the *Amen* because, through Him, the purposes of God are established (II Cor. 1:20). In the Book of Revelation, God's purpose is to pour out His wrath by the hand of His Son, Who is the Judge of all the earth (John 5:27 cf. Rev. 6:16,17). Amen—so be it!

Those who have the misconception that divine justice is a thing of the past need only read the Book of Revelation to see how far afield they have gone. The reference to Christ being the "faithful and true Witness" serves a twofold purpose. For the Kingdom saints who respond to Him in faith, He will be faithful and true to His Word and bring them into the blessings of the Kingdom. But He will also honor His Word to all those who reject Him and blaspheme His holy name. He will be a faithful and true Witness *against* them in the Day of Judgment, as foretold in the Scriptures.

Christ also identifies Himself as "the Beginning of the creation of God." The term "Beginning" here, according to Thayer, has the idea of "origin." We are to understand that Christ is the *originator* of creation. All things, whether visible or invisible, came forth from His hand in the beginning

(Col. 1:16,17), which speaks of His sovereignty. The significance of this cannot be overstated for this reason: what Adam lost in the fall, Christ will one day redeem back to Himself (Rom. 8:20-24). The recovery and restoration of creation will begin with the unfolding of the Tribulation and conclude with the new heaven and new earth.

INDECISION

> "I know thy works, that thou art neither cold nor hot: I would thou wert cold or hot. So then because thou art lukewarm, and neither cold nor hot, I will spue thee out of my mouth" (Rev. 3:15,16).

"Former President Ronald Reagan once had an aunt who took him to a cobbler for a pair of new shoes. The cobbler asked young Reagan, 'Do you want square toes or round toes?' Unable to decide, Reagan didn't answer, so the cobbler gave him a few days.

"Several days later the cobbler saw Reagan on the street and asked him again what kind of toes he wanted on his shoes. Reagan still couldn't decide, so the shoemaker replied, 'Well, come by in a couple of days. Your shoes will be ready.' When the future President did so, he found one square-toed and one round-toed shoe! 'This will teach you to never let people make decisions for you,' the cobbler said to his indecisive customer.

"'I learned right then and there,' Reagan said later, 'if you don't make your own decisions, someone else will.'"[1]

If they fail to repent, the indecision of those at Laodicea will have eternal consequences. Those who make up this assembly are said to be "lukewarm," which is obnoxious in the sight of God . We, too, find it to be deplorable in our daily lives. We like our cold drinks cold and our hot drinks piping hot. If either one becomes lukewarm, we find it distasteful.

The Lord preferred that this assembly either be *cold* or *hot*, but not lukewarm, simply because lukewarm sounds an uncertain trumpet. If a church is stone cold dead spiritually, it is clearly identified as such. It is obvious there's no life there; consequently, true believers avoid it. When Martin Luther perceived that the church of his day was corrupt (cold), he stepped away from it, which launched the Protestant Reformation. Of course, when a local church stands without apology for the truth and is on fire for the things of the Lord (hot), those who are uninterested in spiritual things steer clear of it. On the other hand, the spiritually-minded believer praises God and looks forward to being in attendance to hear the Word. The point is that everyone knows where these assemblies stand. Concerning the lukewarm assembly, well, that's another story altogether, as we are going to see.

In regard to being *lukewarm*, historically, there were numerous times in Israel's past that she was guilty of this type of mediocre behavior. One such period was in the days of King Ahab, who sowed the seeds of idol-worship among the children of Israel. Of course, it wasn't long before the people were persuaded to worship Baal. *He's God*; that's what they were led to believe. Ahab and those who followed him in this were guilty of blatantly breaking the first two commandments of God.

"Thou shalt have no other gods before me" (Ex. 20:3).

"Thou shalt not make unto thee any graven image" (Ex. 20:4a).

These commandments didn't deter Ahab and his wife Jezebel, who was the real power behind the throne. In fact, Jezebel had all the prophets of God systematically hunted down and killed; she then replaced them with the 450 prophets of Baal who frequently ate at the Queen's table. While

God's patience is limitless and infinite, He does not extend it indefinitely. Enter Elijah! God sends the prophet Elijah to King Ahab with the following message:

> "As the LORD God of Israel liveth, before whom I stand, there shall not be dew nor rain these years, but according to my word" (I Kings 17:1).

Notice that it wasn't just a few months, but *years*, the end result being a severe drought and famine. The land would become a dust bowl. As you can see, God has inventive ways of getting the attention of those who are inattentive of His will. After three and one-half years (James 5:17), the people were undoubtedly beginning to wonder where Baal was. Since Baal was nowhere to be found, Elijah stepped forward with a proposal. If you think the "Most Wanted" list originated with the FBI, you would be wrong, because Jezebel had her own "Most Wanted" list and Elijah was at the top of it.

While Jezebel was probably out coordinating the efforts to have Elijah killed, he was standing in the King's court to let Ahab know, in no uncertain terms, that the idol worship he introduced into Israel was the reason for the famine throughout the land. Ahab and Jezebel were the ones, along with their false prophets, who had turned the people's hearts away from Jehovah. Since they had convinced themselves that Baal was God, Elijah offered this challenge:

> "How long halt ye between two opinions? If the LORD be God, follow Him: but if Baal, then follow him. And the people answered him not a word" (I Kings 18:21).

It is important to note here that all the people who were present at Mt. Carmel **"answered him not a word."** Why? They desired to remain neutral. In their heart of hearts they wanted to believe Jehovah was God, but it was more popular to believe that Baal was God. They were **lukewarm** like the Laodiceans will be!

To determine once and for all exactly who the true and living God was—Baal or Jehovah—Elijah offered a proposal. The 450 prophets of Baal were to take an ox and cut it up and place it on wood on the altar at Mt. Carmel, but they were not to place any fire under it; Elijah would do likewise. Then they were to call on Baal and Elijah would call on Jehovah, and the One Who answered with fire to consume the sacrifice would be declared God (I Kings 18:22-25).

According to *Unger's Bible Dictionary*, Baal was known as the storm god, a god who had power over nature; therefore, it would seem to be a small matter for him to send a bolt of lightning to consume the sacrifice and declare himself unequivocally to be God. However, the prophets and priests of Baal prayed and danced around the altar and mutilated themselves for hours, but the heavens were silent!

Seeing that the altar of the LORD had been destroyed years earlier due to Baal worship, Elijah repaired it placing 12 stones on it, each one represented one of the twelve tribes of Israel. After he completed this task, he laid the pieces of the cut-up oxen upon the altar. He then ordered that 12 barrels of water be poured over the altar, literally drenching it. At that point, Elijah lifted his voice to the LORD:

> "Hear me, O LORD, hear me, that this people may know that thou art the LORD God, and that thou hast turned their heart back again. Then the fire of the LORD fell, and consumed the burnt-sacrifice, and the wood, and the stones, and the dust, and licked up the water that was in the trench. And when all the people saw it, they fell on their faces: and they said, The LORD, He is the God; the LORD, He is the God" (I Kings 18:37-39).

Wouldn't you love to have seen the faces of the prophets of Baal that day? It gives new meaning to the words *shell shocked!* For leading the children of Israel astray, the 450 prophets of Baal all were slain that day. Case closed: Jehovah is God!

Returning to the Book of Revelation, the Lord is sounding a similar warning to Israel: "Turn or burn," as Charles Spurgeon once said. The lukewarm church is a lethal blend of *outward* devotion to God and religious fervor. It has a form of godliness but in reality it is a citadel of pomp and circumstance. It is merely an empty shell. The lukewarm church is extremely dangerous because it gives those who are joined to it a false sense of security, similar to Catholicism. This is especially true of those who will be newcomers to the faith that would naturally conclude this to be the norm.

The assembly at Laodicea will be made up primarily of religious unbelievers who will find themselves in danger of being "spued out" of the Lord's mouth, a clear reference to His displeasure with this assembly. This has nothing to do with the loss of their salvation, seeing that the majority of them never possessed salvation to begin with; rather it has all to do with the loss of their position of blessing to be a light to the world. This assembly had drifted far from their covenant relationship with God, which needs first to be restored before they can proceed.

AN HONEST EVALUATION

"Because thou sayest, I am rich, and increased with goods, and have need of nothing; and knowest not that thou art wretched, and miserable, and poor, and blind, and naked" (Rev. 3:17).

When John introduces the seven churches in Asia, the Son of Man is standing in the midst of them, but by the time we come to the church at Laodicea the Lord is standing *outside* the door of this assembly (Rev. 3:20). Sadly, we see that wealth and prosperity will be their god. They will be rich, materially, and have everything the heart could ever desire in relation to the church. By their own admission, they will "have need of nothing." The edifice they will erect to worship in will give new meaning to extravagance. Apparently many things within this magnificent structure will be overlaid with *gold* after the manner of the temple. People will flock to this assembly simply to be able to say they attend there.

This wouldn't be the first time that prosperity is confused with the Lord's blessing. If the Lord's favor is measured by materialism and opulence, then Mormonism and Roman Catholicism would be a demonstration of God's blessing, which we certainly know is not the case since both of these are false religions. God has always done His greatest work through remnants, little flocks, and the church in the house, most of whom labored in poverty (Rev. 2:9).

The church at Laodicea will be characterized by a spirit of Pharisaism. They will be so consumed with keeping up outward appearances that they will have no interest whatsoever in reaching the poor and needy with the gospel. Affluence has no welcome for the disadvantaged; after all, there's an image to keep up!

The Lord says of this assembly that they are "wretched, and miserable, and poor, and blind, and naked." In short, for the most part, those who will make up this assembly are said to be *spiritually dead*. In this context, if they are "blind," then they are in spiritual darkness. If they are "naked," it can only mean they are not clothed in the righteousness of God. As it was in the case of Cain, the Lord has the solution to the problem of their unbelief.

"I counsel thee to buy of me gold tried in the fire, that thou mayest be rich; and white raiment, that thou mayest be clothed, and that the shame of thy nakedness do not appear; and anoint thine eyes with eyesalve, that thou mayest see" (Rev. 3:18).

Those who aspire to be a Christian counselor need to note carefully how the Lord goes directly to the heart of the problem. They were to buy of Him gold tried in the fire. All the gold in Solomon's mines could not make them right with God; they had to come to Christ! Gold speaks of divine glory in the Scriptures; therefore, if they placed their trust in Christ as their Messiah, it would bring glory to God, who provided the once-for-all sacrifice for their sins. This means they would become the beneficiaries of *true riches*, spiritual riches, which include being clothed in garments of salvation. They would be clothed in white raiment, and white, of course, symbolizes the righteousness of God. This is emblematic of their right *standing* with God.

In regard to their *state*, the Lord instructs them to apply eyesalve to their eyes. You will recall the time the Lord anointed the eyes of a blind man with clay and instructed him to go to the pool of Siloam to wash. Not only did the man receive his natural sight upon *believing* on Him Who healed him, he received spiritual sight as well (John 9:1-35). This is also the Lord's will for those who would respond to Him in faith at Laodicea. He wants them to apply the Word of God to their lives, that the eyes of their understanding might be opened to the blessings of the coming Kingdom.

"As many as I love, I rebuke and chasten: be zealous therefore, and repent" (Rev. 3:19).

Although there may well be a small number of true believers who will confuse religious activity with spirituality, the foregoing passages substantiate that the vast majority in this assembly are going to be unsaved.

Once again, we cannot overemphasize the fact that God will be dealing with Israel nationally in the coming Tribulation. In time past, God *loved* Israel, He *rebuked* her and *chastened* her, and even called her to *repentance*; after all, they were His people. But we must always remember that not all within the chosen nation were saved. As the Scriptures clearly teach, "For they are not all Israel, which are of Israel" (Rom. 9:6b). The rebuke and call to repentance then is primarily intended for the unbelieving in the assembly at Laodicea.

> "Behold, I stand at the door, and knock: if any man hear my voice, and open the door, I will come in to him, and will sup with him, and he with me" (Rev. 3:20).

If there is one verse in the arsenal of the evangelist that is the capstone of his gospel presentation, this would be the passage. It goes something like this: "Dear sinner friend, if you will simply open the door of your heart and receive the Lord Jesus by faith, He will come in and save you from your sins, give you the free gift of eternal life, and take you to heaven."

Christian artists have also sought to capture this moment by portraying the lowly Savior standing at a door, which represents the door of the sinner's heart. If you look closely, there is no latch on the Lord's side of the door; therefore, it must be opened by the sinner, from his side, so the Lord can enter. This sounds positively romantic, but this passage has absolutely nothing to do with salvation in the administration of Grace. Although He will save to the uttermost those who come to Him, we must remember that the Son of Man is not presented as the Savior in the Book of Revelation, but rather as the Judge of all the earth.

This is confirmed by the fact that the Lord is standing at the door of this assembly, giving them one last opportunity before it's too late. He is standing there as the Judge (James 5:9). The plea, *"if any man hear my voice,"* is to be understood as a general call, first and foremost to those at Laodicea, but to the other assemblies in Asia as well (Rev. 3:22). If they open the door without delay, He will receive them to Himself and include them as participants in the marriage of the Lamb and the wedding feast to follow. If they fail to grant Him admittance, the Judge will break down the door and summarily judge them accordingly.

> "To him that overcometh will I grant to sit with me in my throne, even as I also overcame, and am set down with my Father in his throne. He that hath an ear, let him hear what the Spirit saith unto the churches" (Rev. 3:21,22).

This promise is completely foreign to the Body of Christ. As members of His Body, we are already said to be seated with Christ in the heavenlies where we will rule and reign with Him in the ages to come (Eph. 2:6,7). The overcomers at Laodicea are instead promised to be seated with Christ on the *earth* during the Millennial Kingdom. In that day, Christ will reign on the throne of David in Jerusalem, wonderfully fulfilling the promise given to David (Acts 2:30), and these Tribulation saints will rule and reign with Him (Rev. 2:26,27).

IN SUMMARY

The letter to the Laodiceans is a clinic on the perils of religion. Religion appeals to that which is inherent in man to want to do something to please God. It was introduced in the Garden, when our first parents sewed fig leaves together in an attempt to make themselves acceptable to their Creator. The experiment failed miserably because, without *faith*, it is impossible to please God.

Those who have had a religious upbringing are far more difficult to reach for Christ, simply because they believe their devotion to God and religious practices will secure them a place in heaven. It is far easier to reach someone who has never darkened a church door than the religionist.

7

The Throne Room of God

"After this I looked, and, behold, a door was opened in heaven: and the first voice which I heard was as it were of a trumpet talking with me; which said, Come up hither, and I will show thee things which must be hereafter."

—*Revelation 4:1*

SETTING THE RECORD STRAIGHT

Most commentators who have written on the Book of Revelation are like sheep following one another down the wrong path. Their claim that John is writing to members of the Body of Christ in the first four chapters is not only inconsistent with the context, but an outright failure to rightly divide the Word of truth. Needless to say, it has caused a great deal of confusion in the Church today.

If we carefully examine the terminology and phraseology of the first four chapters of Revelation, it is clear that God's prophetic program is in view, the heart of which is the earthly ministry of Christ and the Kingdom gospel. A *brief comparison* of the two programs of God makes this crystal clear.

"The Revelation of Jesus Christ, which God gave unto Him, to show unto His servants things which must shortly come to pass; and He sent and signified it by His angel unto His servant John" (Rev. 1:1).

In the Book of Revelation, we have the revelation of Jesus Christ according to *prophecy,* wherein Christ is revealed as the *Judge of all the earth*. The Apostle John, who was one of the twelve apostles of the *circumcision* (Israel), is the one who received this revelation about the Son of Man (Rev. 1:3 cf. 1:12-18).

> "But I [Apostle Paul] certify you, brethren, that the gospel which was preached of me is not after man. For I neither received it of man, neither was I taught it, but by the revelation of Jesus Christ" (Gal. 1:11,12).

In Paul's epistles, we have the revelation of Jesus Christ according to the *Mystery*, where Christ is presented as the *Head* of the Church, the Body of Christ. The Apostle Paul, the apostle of the *uncircumcision* (Gentiles), was the one who received this revelation from the Lord of glory (Rom. 11:13 cf. 16:25).

> "And hath made us kings and priests unto God and His Father; to Him be glory and dominion forever and ever. Amen" (Rev. 1:6).

In the Book of Revelation, John's readers have been made *kings* and *priests*, a common designation for believing Israelites (Ex. 19:6; I Pet. 2:9; Rev. 5:10).

> "Let a man so account of us, as of the ministers of Christ, and stewards of the mysteries of God. Moreover it is required in stewards, that a man be found faithful" (I Cor. 4:1,2).
>
> "Now then we are ambassadors for Christ..." (II Cor. 5:20).

In the Gentile epistles, Paul never refers to the members of the Body of Christ as kings and priests, and for good reason. We are the *ambassadors* of Christ who represent Him in His royal exile from the earth. Paul also calls us the *stewards* of the Mysteries of God. So then, we are to understand that we're God's ambassadors and stewards today.

"I know the blasphemy of them which say they are
Jews, and are not, but are the synagogue of Satan"
(Rev. 2:9b).

The *synagogue*, in biblical times, was a facility where
the Scriptures were read and taught. In the passage just
quoted the synagogue at Smyrna is said to be corrupted by
those who claimed to be Jews, but in actuality were followers of Satan. The reference to the synagogue in the above
passage is Jewish through and through (Luke 4:14-21).

> "The churches of Asia salute you. Aquila and Pris-
> cilla salute you much in the Lord, with the church that
> is in their house" (I Cor. 16:19).

> "And to our beloved Apphia, and Archippus our fel-
> lowsoldier, and to the church in thy house" (Phile. 1:2).

The Apostle Paul never uses the term *synagogue* in
any of his epistles. He reveals that the Gentiles met in
their *homes* to study the Scriptures. Therefore, the most
common meeting place for believers at that time was the
church in their house.

> "Him that overcometh will I make a pillar in the
> temple of my God, and he shall go no more out: and
> I will write upon him the name of my God, and the
> name of the city of my God, which is New Jerusalem,
> which cometh down out of heaven from my God: and I
> will write upon him my new name" (Rev. 3:12).

In the Book of Revelation, the overcomers are promised
a *prominent position in the Millennial Temple*, as they rule
and reign with Christ on the earth. They will have the
honor of receiving a *new name* when they enter the New
Jerusalem in eternity.

> "And hath raised us up together, and made us sit
> together in heavenly places in Christ Jesus: That in
> the ages to come He might show the exceeding riches

of His grace in His kindness toward us through Christ Jesus" (Eph. 2:6,7).

In Paul's epistles, we learn that Paul received a *new* revelation from the Lord that the members of the Body of Christ will be seated with Christ in the heavenlies. We have a *heavenly* hope and calling! Throughout eternity, God is going to show us the exceeding riches of His grace in the heavens.

A SCENE THAT DEFIES EXPLANATION

In Revelation Chapter 4, we come to the first of seven visions in the course of the Day of the Lord. Each of the seven visions has two parts. In the first part, our attention is drawn to heaven, while the second part takes place on the earth, both in direct response to the commands received from the throne of God.

As John looked up, he saw a door was opened in heaven and he received the command from the Lord Jesus Christ, whose voice was like a trumpet, clear and powerful, to "Come up hither." Once again, it is a major dispensational blunder to say this is a reference to John and the Church being caught up to be with the Lord. The prophetic program knows nothing of an event called the Rapture. This particular revelation concerning the Lord's return for the Church was committed only to the Apostle Paul (I Cor. 15:51,52; I Thes. 4:13-18; Phil. 3:14).

The phraseology, "Come up hither," or "Come hither," is a common phrase found in the Book of Revelation (Rev. 4:1; 11:12; 17:1; and 21:9). Three of the four times it's used, John is transported to a new location to view and record new events as his vision unfolds. Here in Revelation 4:1, he is transported to the throne of God, where he is about to learn the source of the coming judgments that will soon befall the earth. Although some theologians, notably Islamic theologians, speak of seven heavens, our Scriptures only teach three heavens, the third being called the heaven of heavens, the very abode of God (Neh. 9:6 cf. II Cor. 12:1-4). All divine action in the future Tribulation clearly originates from the heaven of heavens.

John now prepares to record "the things which shall be hereafter" (Rev. 1:19). The Old Testament and the four Gospel accounts never present a complete chronological order of things to come. John, however, gives us an extensive sequence of events from beginning to end, interwoven with parenthetical sections for additional clarification. He methodically records for us the things that will *come to pass* in the Day of the Lord. The following passages are three examples: "Come up hither, and I will show thee things which must be *hereafter*" (Rev. 4:1), that is, which must be *"after these things;"* "*And after these things* I saw four angels standing on the four corners of the earth, holding the four winds of the earth, that the wind should not blow on the earth" (Rev. 7:1); "*And after these things* I saw another angel come down from heaven, having great power" (Rev. 18:1).

> "And immediately I was in the Spirit: and, behold, a throne was set in heaven, and One sat on the throne. And He that sat was to look upon like a jasper and a sardine stone: and there was a rainbow round about the throne, in sight like unto an emerald" (Rev. 4:2,3).

The first thing that draws John's attention is the throne of God. This is not a throne of grace, neither is it the throne of His glory, nor the Great White Throne. Rather, it is a throne "set" in heaven; that is, set for judgment! The One seated on the throne is God the Father, Who is surrounded by an array of beautiful shades of color. We are able to draw this conclusion safely because we know the Son is *standing* by the throne, in fulfillment of Psalm 7: "Arise,

O LORD, in thine anger." Additionally, we read that the Son, the Lamb of God, is said to have received the seven-sealed scroll from the Father who was seated on the throne (Rev. 5:1-7 cf. 7:9,10).

Even though John was caught away in the Spirit to witness the One Who was seated on the throne, we must bear in mind that he is still a mere mortal. This is why the presence of the Father and His glory are veiled in brilliant hues, for "No man hath seen God at any time; the only begotten Son, which is in the bosom of the Father, He hath declared Him" (John 1:18).

It is significant that the Spirit of God makes mention of jasper and sardine stones. The jasper stone was clear as crystal (Rev. 21:11), similar to our diamond, while on the other hand, the sardine or sardius was a well-known red gem in biblical times. Today it is called a ruby. Both were transparent! So we are to understand that the Father appeared to John as a brilliant light diffused through these two gems. God is light! Thus the scene before him is utterly awe-inspiring.

But there is another reason for mentioning these two stones. In the Book of Exodus, we learn that they were found on the breastplate of the high priest in accordance with a special revelation from God. There were twelve different stones on the breastplate, each of which represented one of the twelve tribes of Israel. The first and last stones on the high priest's breastplate were the sardius and the jasper (Ex. 28:17-20). Therefore, John's reference to them in the vision teaches us that God has not forgotten the chosen nation. Israel will, once again, be the apple of His eye in the Day of the Lord.

The twelve stones in the breastplate were placed there according to the birth order of the children of Israel (Gen.

49:2-28). The sardius represented the tribe of Reuben. Reuben, of course, was the firstborn of Jacob. The name Reuben means "See, a son,"[1] which speaks beautifully of Christ, Who is the only begotten Son. Benjamin was the last born of Israel; consequently, the jasper represented the tribe that bore his name. Benjamin's name means "son of my right hand," which is a position of favor.[2] This also speaks of Christ, Who is the Son of God, He too is seated at the right hand of His Father. So then, the appearance of the Father seated on the throne is to be viewed here in relation to Israel.

It was probably difficult for John to take in everything when he initially arrived in heaven, but as he studied the scene, he observed an emerald rainbow that encircled the throne of God. Our first introduction to the rainbow was after the flood, when God promised Noah He would never again destroy the earth with water (Gen. 9:8-17). This promise was made in conjunction with a blood sacrifice that Noah made after he disembarked from the Ark (Gen. 8:20-22). Both rainbows, the one in the days of Noah and the one John saw in glory, have a direct relationship to the *earth*. The bow surrounding the throne in heaven was a lush green color, which, as we know, is one of the predominant colors of the earth.

The rainbow encircling the throne is a symbol of the promise that God will one day redeem the earth to Himself, which is the overarching subject of prophecy (Ex. 19:5,6; Psa. 24:1 cf. 104:5). This too is based on a blood sacrifice, the once-for-all sacrifice of God's dear Son. Despite the terrible judgments the earth will pass through, God will not destroy it. After the Millennium, but prior to the eternal state, He will *restore* His creation to its original state of perfection (Psa. 104:5 cf. Rev. 21:1). Both rainbows remind us that God keeps His promises.

WHO ARE THE TWENTY-FOUR ELDERS?

"And round about the throne were four and twenty seats: and upon the seats I saw four and twenty elders sitting, clothed in white raiment; and they had on their heads crowns of gold" (Rev. 4:4).

Exactly who are the twenty-four elders seated around the throne of God? To say this has long been debated by capable Bible teachers would probably be an understatement. Two of the more prominent interpretations held by commentators are as follows:

1. Perhaps the most popular view is that they are representatives of the Church, the Body of Christ. The problem with this position is that it confuses the two programs of God—Prophecy and Mystery. The events being unfolded before us by the Apostle John are unmistakably connected to the prophetic program. In addition, we know that according to the Mystery, we are seated with Christ who is enthroned "**Far above** all principality, and power, and might, and dominion, and every name that is named, not only in this world, but also in that which is to come" (Eph. 1:21 cf. 2:6).

2. Others believe these twenty-four elders are representatives of God's earthly program, specifically, the 12 patriarchs and the 12 apostles of the Kingdom. To support this view, it is pointed out that the twenty-four elders are clothed in white raiment (the attire of the saints) and they cast their crowns of gold, which they received as a reward, at the feet of the Father (Rev. 4:10). This position, at least, is more consistent with the Scriptures and is certainly well worth consideration.

This second view, though, poses a major problem given that the 12 patriarchs and 12 apostles would have to be already resurrected from the dead, judged, and have received their rewards, since they are all wearing victory crowns. However, the heavenly scene here in Chapter 4 takes place at a point in time *prior to* God unleashing His wrath upon the earth. Now we know that the first resurrection, when the patriarchs and apostles will be raised, doesn't occur until after the Second Coming of Christ (Matt. 8:11; Rev. 19:11-14 cf. Rev. 20:6), so the twenty-four elders can't possibly be the patriarchs and apostles.

We believe the twenty-four elders are a heavenly, angelic priesthood. This is one of the highest orders of angels, serving under the cherubs as the governors of heavenly worship. John noted that they sit on twenty-four seats or thrones [Gr. *thronos*], which coincides with the *heavenly* thrones the Lord brought into existence at creation. "For by Him were all things created, that are in heaven, and that are in earth, visible and invisible, whether they be thrones (Gr. *thronos*), or dominions, or principalities, or powers: all things were created by Him, and for Him" (Col. 1:16). These are seats of authority that are occupied by this special class of angels. Due to the dignity of their rank and office, they are called "elders." Interestingly, these angelic elders/priests are *seated* around the throne of God while the heavenly host is always observed as standing (Luke 1:19 cf. Rev. 7:11).

It is essential to remember in this narrative that the earthly tabernacle/temple and its rituals were all patterned *after* the heavenly (Ex. 25:40; Heb. 8:4,5). So when King David divided the priests who led Israel in worship into twenty-four courses, that was based on the twenty-four elders who lead the heavenly host in worship (I Chron. 24:3-5 cf. Rev. 4:4,10). Additionally, the main garment of the high priest in Israel was made of fine white linen; this was true of Aaron's sons as well who served as priests (Ex. 28:2-5 cf. Rev. 4:4). The high priest also wore a crown of gold on his head, which should not to be confused with the royal diadem—the kingly crown (Ex. 28:36-38; 29:6). All these details were specifically patterned after the angelic priesthood in heaven called the twenty-four elders. As a side bar, we normally associate "white raiment" with the saints in the Word of God, but it is not uncommon for the angels also to be clothed in white, which is noteworthy of this angelic priesthood around the throne (Matt. 28:2,3; John 20:12 cf. Rev. 4:4).

But what about Revelation 5:8-10, where the twenty-four elders sing of their redemption? Doesn't this demonstrate that these elders are redeemed men? Not necessarily! We will address this question at length in the next chapter. In the meantime, we leave you with a final thought on this topic. According to Revelation 11:16-19, these angelic elders *differentiate* themselves from the prophets and the saints for whom they intercede during the course of the Tribulation (see Rev. 7:13,14).

> "And out of the throne proceeded lightnings and thunderings and voices: and there were seven lamps of fire burning before the throne, which are the seven Spirits of God" (Rev. 4:5).

The primary purpose for John being transported to heaven was that he and those who will endure the Tribulation would understand the *source* of the judgments that will come. There is absolutely no question whatsoever that the judgments will proceed from the throne of God. Interestingly, it is no longer a throne of grace, as Paul presents it in his epistles, but a throne of judgment.

The apostle's account in this passage of the lightning, thunder, and voices substantiates this for us. In time past, when God wanted to show His displeasure against sin, He did so by causing brilliant lightning to slice through the atmosphere like a knife. Simultaneously, He caused thunder to shake the earth to get everyone's undivided attention, followed by heavenly voices which were unnerving. A good example is when God gave the Law to Israel; He wanted His people to understand fully the seriousness of sin:

> "And it came to pass on the third day in the morning, that there were thunders and lightnings, and a thick cloud upon the mount, and the voice of the trumpet exceeding loud; so that all the people that was in the camp trembled" (Ex. 19:16).

God's enemies also got the message loud and clear. When the Philistines drew near to do battle with God's chosen people, "the LORD thundered with a great thunder on that day upon the Philistines, and discomfited them; and they were smitten before Israel" (I Sam. 7:10). In the coming Day of the Lord, the cup of the world's immorality and rebellion will be overflowing. God will respond in the fierceness of His anger and pour out His wrath upon this world of unbelief (Rev. 16:17-21). It will be the day of His vengeance!

The "seven lamps of fire burning before the throne, which are the seven Spirits of God" of Revelation 4:5 will play a key role in the execution of God's wrath upon the earth (Rev. 5:6 cf. 8:2). As we saw in Revelation Chapter 1, these are seven angelic messengers of the highest order who stand before God day and night to carry out the counsel of His will. Chief among them is Michael the Archangel (Dan. 12:1). These are the seven torches of God, emblematic of preparation for battle, as in the days of Gideon (Judges 7:16,20). These flames will illuminate the darkness and expose the gross evil of this world. They are represented in the earthly tabernacle/temple by the seven-branched golden candlestick, with its lamps, which were never permitted to be extinguished (Num. 8:1-4).

THE FOUR BEASTS

"And before the throne there was a sea of glass like unto crystal: and in the midst of the throne, and round about the throne, were four beasts full of eyes before and behind. And the first beast was like a lion, and the second beast like a calf, and the third beast had a face as a man, and the fourth beast was like a flying eagle" (Rev. 4:6,7).

The lives and affairs of men are like a troubled sea, but the scene before us here is one of tranquility in spite of the impending storms. The *brass laver* in the tabernacle, where the priests purified themselves, and the "molten sea" in Solomon's temple corresponds to this sea of glass in heaven (Ex. 30:18 cf. II Chron. 4:2-6). The fact that the sea is *like* a crystal speaks of two things. First and foremost, God is separate from His creation. He transcends it! He is *pure*! Second, we are reminded that heaven is a real place that is teeming with activity. It is a place of *realities*, as we will one day see for ourselves.

Around about the throne, as John tells us, there were posted "four beasts." In the original language, *beast* is the Greek word *zoon*, which denotes *a living being*. This isn't the first time these living creatures are brought to our attention in the Word of God. The prophet Ezekiel identifies these four living ones as the cherubs who are protectors of God's holiness (Ezek. 10:20-22). We also know they are created beings. Originally there were five cherubs, but one fell by reason of pride over his wisdom and beauty and was cast out of the third heaven by God. This, of course, was none other than Lucifer himself. Both Ezekiel and the Apostle John give very similar descriptions of the cherubs, but they are not identical, probably because they were viewing them from different vantage points and under different circumstances.

It is significant that the number of the cherubs is four, which connects them directly to creation. The number four is prominently stamped on God's creation of the earth:[3]

- 4 elements—earth, air, fire, and water
- 4 points of the compass—north, south, east, and west
- 4 divisions of the day—morning, noon, evening, and midnight
- 4 seasons of the year—spring, summer, autumn, and winter

The first reference to the cherubim is found in Genesis 3:24, where they are found guarding the Tree of Life in the Garden of Eden. Had Adam and Eve eaten of this forbidden tree, they would have lived eternally in a sinful state. So we are first introduced to the cherubim immediately after sin entered God's creation, and now again as God is about to redeem it back to Himself at the consummation of all things here in the Book of Revelation. It is noteworthy that their four images were found in the tabernacle/temple on the earth where two faced one another on the mercy seat and two were woven into the tapestry of the veil (Ex. 25:18-20; 26:31). This too follows the pattern of heaven, where there are four cherubs continually in the presence of God.

> "And in the midst of the throne, and round about the throne, were four beasts full of eyes before and behind. And the first beast was like a lion, and the second beast like a calf, and the third beast had a face as a man, and the fourth beast was like a flying eagle" (Rev. 4:6b,7).

Just as the Lord Jesus Christ is presented in *symbolic* language in Chapter 5, as a slain lamb with seven horns, the same is true here in Chapter 4 of the cherubim that are stationed at the throne of God. That they are "full of eyes

147

before and behind" is simply an indication that they have the ability to view the past and look forward into the future.

The appearance of the first living being was like "A lion which is strongest among beasts, and turneth not away for any" (Prov. 30:30). The lion is fearless; it never backs down from danger; it always stands its ground. The same is true of the cherubim who are the guardians of God's holiness. None dare challenge their regal *authority*, as seen in the Garden where they stood guard with a flaming sword. They were prepared on a moment's notice to defend the sanctity of the Garden of God where the LORD often appeared (Gen. 3:8,9,24).

The second living being was like a calf. We believe this to be the "calf" of the ox described in Ezekiel 1:10. The Scriptures say, "Thou shalt not muzzle the ox when he treadeth out the corn" (Deut. 25:4). The ox always renders *patient service* for his master. This can also be said of the cherubim who faithfully serve the Lord God Almighty. In the Garden of Eden, they guarded the Tree of Life with a flaming sword. And in John's vision, when the Lamb of God opened the first seal, launching the judgments of the Tribulation, it was one of the cherubs who told John to "come and see" what was about to occur on the earth (Rev. 6:1). None dare question their faithful *service*.

We note the third living being "had a face as a man." Since man is created in the image of God, he is endowed with intelligence and therefore, has the ability to reason. "Come now, and let us reason together, saith the LORD" (Isa. 1:18a). We are to understand, then, that the cherubim are also *intelligent* beings who are able to exercise will. In fact, before his fall, Lucifer was commended by God, that he "[sealed] up the sum, full of wisdom, and perfect in beauty" (Ezek. 28:11-15). In other words, the cherub known as

Lucifer was the pinnacle of God's angelic creation, who apparently led the host of heaven in song and worship. In like manner, the four living beings give glory, honor, and thanks to God for who He is and what He has accomplished in creation (Rev. 4:9-11). Let all marvel at their God-given *intelligence*.

Finally, the fourth living being "was like a flying eagle." The eagle is well-known for its strength, keen sight, and graceful movement as it soars through the skies. The Scriptures say of the mother eagle that she "stirreth up her nest, fluttereth over her young, spreadeth abroad her wings, taketh them, beareth them on her wings" (Deut. 32:11). The reference to this cherub flying like an eagle conveys the idea of *swiftness*. They are able to move from place to place effortlessly in a moment of time (Ezek. 1:14 cf. Rev. 4:8). Let all bear witness to their *agility*.

HE WHO IS WORTHY OF WORSHIP

> "And the four beasts had each of them six wings about him; and they were full of eyes within: and they rest not day and night, saying, Holy, holy, holy, Lord God Almighty, which was, and is, and is to come. And when those beasts give glory and honor and thanks to Him that sat on the throne, Who liveth for ever and ever" (Rev. 4:8,9).

While many will be chagrined to learn that angels don't have wings, there are two distinct classes of angelic beings that do and they hold supreme positions over all of the heavenly host. They are the cherubim and the seraphim, which both have six wings (Isa. 6:2-7; Rev. 4:8). That cherubs have wings is also confirmed in the Book of Exodus, where God instructed Moses to prepare two cherubim with outstretched *wings* to cover the mercy seat (Ex. 25:20). And we know that seraphim have wings because a seraph *flew* into the presence of the prophet Isaiah to purge his unclean lips (Isa. 6:5-7).

It is clear from the Scriptures that the seraphim hover *above* the throne of God where they acknowledge to one another that the Lord of hosts is holy (Isa. 6:1-3). The cherubim, on the other hand, are described as being positioned *around* the throne, where they faithfully perform the administration of divine government, of which they are representatives. That "they were full of eyes within" speaks of how they are able to look "inward upon themselves and into the nature of things, and able to direct their ways and administrations with unlimited penetration and discretion."[4]

The six wings of the cherubs here in Revelation testify of their unceasing activity, for "they rest not day and night, saying, Holy, holy, holy, Lord God Almighty, which was, and is, and is to come." Since heaven is eternally day because God is light, John's reference here to "day and night" is in connection to the *earth*.

One of the purposes of the cherubim is to declare and safeguard the holiness of God. God is holy! He is pure, morally blameless, and set apart from sin. In relation to His dealings with man in time past, God Almighty "was" holy. As He prepares to execute His wrath against man's sin in the Tribulation, which He is perfectly justified in doing, He "is" holy. In the Millennial Kingdom that "is to come," He will be holy. When Isaiah, whom we know to have been a very godly man, witnessed the holiness of God in a vision, he declared, "Woe is me! For I am undone; because I am a man of unclean lips" (Isa. 6:5). We fear that many believers today do not fully understand the holiness of God, or they would have more of a desire to live a godly life in Christ Jesus.

> "The four and twenty elders fall down before Him
> that sat on the throne, and worship Him that liveth
> for ever and ever, and cast their crowns before the
> throne, saying, Thou art worthy, O Lord, to receive
> glory and honor and power: for Thou hast created all
> things, and for thy pleasure they are and were created"
> (Rev. 4:10,11).

Because the four cherubs and the twenty-four elders
owe their existence to the Creator Who created all things
in heaven and earth, they give Him all the honor, and glory,
and praise that are rightfully due Him. We see this also
exhibited in the actions of the twenty-four elders, who cast
their priestly crowns before the throne as they all bow in
humble adoration to the One seated on the throne. He
is worthy to be worshipped as the Creator because He is
sovereign! Daniel writes:

> "And all the inhabitants of the earth are reputed
> as nothing: and He doeth according to His will in the
> army of heaven, and among the inhabitants of the
> earth: and none can stay His hand, or say unto Him,
> What doest Thou?" (Dan. 4:35).

In addition to His holiness, the Lord is worthy to be worshipped because He merely spoke and worlds came into
being. He did so *ex nihilo*; that is, out of nothing came
something when He spoke in His almighty power. He is the
One who flung the stars that dot the night sky into space.
He is One who designed the complexities of the human
body that, to this day, baffle medical science—which just
recently discovered intricate structures *within* the human
cell. He is the One Who wove the blazing red color and
glorious aroma into the beautiful azalea that blooms in the
spring. He is the One Who knows you by name—who loves
you! Who knows what burdens you are bearing. Who has

provided salvation for your lost soul. He is the One Who is above all others! Amen!

All things were created by Him, and for Him, contrary to the thinking of the unbelieving evolutionist who is convinced that man evolved from a slime pit in the dateless past. Unless he turns from this lie and believes the gospel, he will perish along with his godless theory. Notice in verses 10 and 11 above that all things have been created according to His good pleasure (will). Until an individual acknowledges God to be the Creator and that Christ died for his sins, he will wander aimlessly through life without hope or purpose. Man was created to honor and glorify God. This is his purpose in life, pure and simple, but before he can realize this, he must first respond to God in faith.

As this passage plainly states, all things "are" created by God according to His will; in short, everything and everyone owe their existence to God. And the twenty-four elders add, "And 'were' created"—past tense. God created all things in six, literal, 24-hour days in the beginning. Creation was a once-for-all act. No aspect of it can be reproduced by men or angels. Man will never possess the power, knowledge, authority, or ability to create something *ex nihilo*. He can only work with and manage what God has already called into existence.

The time of the end has come! What was once lost in the Fall is soon to be redeemed by God. The scene before us in Revelation Chapter 4 is a celebration of the redemption of creation.

8

Worthy Is the Lamb

> "And I saw in the right hand of Him that sat on the throne a book written within and on the backside, sealed with seven seals. And I saw a strong angel proclaiming with a loud voice, Who is worthy to open the book, and to loose the seals thereof?"
>
> —*Revelation 5:1,2*

THE BOOK WITHIN THE BOOK

Most times the chapter divisions in the Scriptures are very helpful, but occasionally they disrupt the continuity of the narrative. We have before us a classic case in point. Notice that Chapter 5 begins with the conjunction, "And," which directly ties what is stated here in verse one to the previous chapter. So the heavenly vision of the throne room of God that we were introduced to in Chapter 4 continues uninterrupted through the fifth chapter of Revelation.

The calling of the Apostle John up into heaven had a twofold purpose. First and foremost was to reveal to him the *source* of the coming judgments, as we noted earlier. We are left with no doubt whatsoever that they will proceed from the hand of God as He speaks to this world in His wrath (Rev. 6:17). But there was another reason John was summoned to the throne of God that is found here in the message of the book that is sealed with seven seals.

As John marveled at the awe-inspiring scene of worship he was privileged to witness, he observed there was a "book" in the right hand of the Father. In biblical times, *books* were in the form of scrolls that were usually rolled up tightly to preserve their message (Ezek. 2:9). It wasn't until the 2nd century A.D. that the *codex* came into existence, a simple form of a book, with pages, similar to what we would hold in our hand today. The unusual thing about this specific scroll was that John observed that it had writing on both sides of the parchment. Normally the message was only written on the inside of the scroll, so as to protect it. Another unique feature of this book was that it had seven seals that could only be broken by someone with the authority to do so.

The fact that the scroll had a message written on both sides simply means that the revelation it contained was extensive and complete. Ezekiel and Daniel, both of whom were post-exile prophets, were permitted to gaze upon the content of the book before it was sealed. Ezekiel reveals that the Lord spread the scroll before him "and it was written within and without: and there was written therein lamentations, and mourning, and woe" (Ezek. 2:10). When Daniel inquired as to when the events covered in the scroll would be fulfilled, he was instructed to "shut up the words, and seal the book...for the words are closed up and sealed till the time of the end" (Dan. 12:4,9). The same scroll that was shut and sealed by Daniel is the one about to be opened in John's vision, for the appointed "time of the end" has come.

John noted that the scroll was sealed with seven seals—seven, of course, being the number of *completeness* and perfection. Apparently the seals were arranged in such a manner that only one seal could be broken at a time. Once the revelation contained therein is fulfilled, the next seal is broken in succession. This is confirmed for us in Chapter 6:

"And I saw when the Lamb opened *one* of the seals, and I heard, as it were the noise of thunder, one of the four beasts saying, Come and see" (Rev. 6:1). This is followed by a major event.

"And when He had opened the *second seal,* I heard the second beast say, Come and see" (Rev. 6:3). This is also followed by a major event.

"And when He had opened the *third seal,* I heard the third beast say, Come and see" (Rev. 6:5), etc. In this case too, opening the seal is followed by a major event, as is the case with all seven seals.

As John was contemplating the significance of the scroll in the right hand of the Father, he "saw a strong angel proclaiming with a loud voice, Who is worthy to open the book, and to loose the seals thereof?" Because the angel Gabriel was instrumental in imparting the revelation of the "end times" in the days of Daniel (Dan. 9:21-27), he is probably also the one who asks the question, "Who is worthy to open the book, and to loose the seals thereof?"

> "And no man in heaven, nor in earth, neither under the earth, was able to open the book, neither to look thereon" (Rev. 5:3).

When a search is made of heaven, and earth, and the nether world of hades, John records for us that no man in any of these realms had the authority to open the book or even "to look thereon." "Neither to look thereon" doesn't mean that no one could look at the scroll, for John himself "saw" it in the right hand of the Father in verse one. Indeed, the host of heaven could see it, but no one was permitted access to it to inspect its contents is the sense. Once it is revealed that no man had the authority to open the book, the apostle writes that he "wept much" (v. 4).

John's weeping wasn't due to his disappointment that he would never understand what the future held; no, it was something far more important. We must bear in mind that John was "in the Spirit"; therefore, the Spirit of God revealed to him the importance of the scroll: that if no one was found worthy to open it, all the promises given to the patriarchs and prophets would fail, and the hope of the saints would not be fulfilled in the coming Kingdom. The very thought of this left the apostle distraught. We rejoice that Someone does step forward Who is worthy to open the seven-sealed scroll, but not just any one.

A DECLARATION OF WORTHINESS

> "And one of the elders saith unto me, Weep not: behold, the Lion of the tribe of Judah, the Root of David, hath prevailed to open the book, and to loose the seven seals thereof" (Rev. 5:5).

After one of the twenty-four elders instructs John to "Weep not," he looks and sees He Who is identified as the "Lion of the tribe of Judah," and the "Root of David." These titles belong exclusively to Christ Who, as we know, is God manifested in the flesh (John 1:1,14). Both titles indicate that, after the Church is removed at the Rapture, God is going to re-establish His relationship with Israel. While these titles have everything to do with Israel in prophecy, they have absolutely nothing to do with the Church, the Body of Christ.

The title, "Lion of the tribe of Judah" refers to the days of Jacob. According to the Scriptures, when Jacob was on the verge of death, he gathered his sons together to bless each of them and tell each one what would befall his descendants, or tribe, in the last days. When he came to his son, Judah, the patriarch prophesied as follows:

> "Judah is a lion's whelp: from the prey, my son, thou art gone up: he stooped down, he couched as a lion, and as an old lion; who shall rouse him up? The scepter shall not depart from Judah, nor a lawgiver from

between his feet, until Shiloh come; and unto Him
shall the gathering of the people be" (Gen. 49:9,10).

Historically, Judah was the tribe of kings. As we trace the
genealogy of our Lord, we learn that He was a descendant of
Judah, which means He had this "lion-type" character. The
lion is well known in the animal kingdom for his authority and power as the king of beasts. Both of these traits
were true of Christ, Who is identified here as the *Lion of the
tribe of Judah*. For example, "When Jesus had ended these
sayings, the people were astonished at His doctrine: For He
taught them as one having authority, and not as the scribes"
(Matt. 7:28,29).

In fulfillment of Jacob's prophecy, we now know that
Christ was *Shiloh*, one meaning of which is *peace-giver*. Not
only was He a peace-giver in His first coming at Bethlehem,
we are to understand that Jacob's prophecy also extends
to Christ's Second Coming, when the Prince of Peace will
return in glory to establish His Kingdom of Righteousness.
You see, the future blessing and restoration of Israel is an
integral part of Christ's inheritance (Psa. 78:71; 94:14). The
reason the Lion of the tribe of Judah has *prevailed* to open
and reveal the contents of the sealed book is because He is
the Root of David. In other words, Christ is the Messiah/
Redeemer Who, through His once-for-all sacrifice, has provided *redemption* in every sense of the word. This will include the Gentiles who will be saved through Israel in that
day. The Apostle Paul reiterates Isaiah's prophecy when he
says, "There shall be a Root of Jesse, and He that shall rise
to reign over the Gentiles; in Him shall the Gentiles trust"
(Rom. 15:12).

It is because Christ "hath prevailed" at Calvary that He
has the authority and the right as the Lion of Judah to
open the scroll and fulfill that which is contained therein.
The ultimate fulfillment of prophecy is the redemption of

Israel, which is about to commence, according to John. It is interesting that Christ will accomplish this through the execution of a series of judgments.

> "And I beheld, and, lo, in the midst of the throne and of the four beasts, and in the midst of the elders, stood a Lamb as it had been slain, having seven horns and seven eyes, which are the seven Spirits of God sent forth into all the earth" (Rev. 5:6).

Although the representations of the "Lion" and the "Lamb" at first appear to be polar opposites, they actually complement one another in this context, as we have already noted in part. While this portion of Scripture is laden with metaphors and symbolic language, we are not left to our own imagination as to the meaning. The Scriptures themselves interpret the metaphors and symbols for us. In the foregoing passage, John uses the metaphor of a "Lamb" to describe the Person and work of Christ. Lambs are submissive to the will of another; the same was true of Christ who submitted Himself to the will of the Father. Lambs are innocent, which was also true of Christ, Who knew no sin. Lambs, in the Old Testament, were led away to the slaughter to atone for the sins of the people. Christ also was led away to the slaughter to redeem us back to God through His precious blood. He is the Lamb of God according to the declaration of John the Baptist (John 1:36). Notice that the Apostle John is careful to record that the Lamb appeared to have been *slain*, which is a clear reference to the wound in His side and the nail prints in His hands that He received at Calvary (John 20:26-29).

We are thankful that the story doesn't end there. John points out that he saw Christ *standing* in the midst of the throne surrounded by the four cherubim and the twenty-four elders. He wants us to see what he saw; that is, there "stood a Lamb." This testifies to the reality that Christ rose

again, having conquered sin and death. As it has been correctly said, "The resurrection of Christ is not a myth, but
a *fact*."[1] Christ's resurrection is proof of His *worthiness* to
receive the scroll from the hand of the Father and open it.

But there's another reason why Christ is said to be
standing in the midst of the throne. This is in fulfillment
of prophecy that was spoken long ago. Every Hebrew child
understood the significance of the Psalms, where many of
these prophecies were recorded.

> "Arise, O LORD, in thine anger, lift up thyself be-
> cause of the rage of mine enemies: and awake for me
> to the judgment that thou hast commanded" (Psa. 7:6).
>
> "O LORD God, to whom vengeance belongeth; O
> God, to whom vengeance belongeth, show thyself. Lift
> up thyself, thou judge of the earth: render a reward to
> the proud" (Psa. 94:1,2).

You will recall that when they stoned Stephen, he saw
heaven open and the Son of Man standing at the right hand
of the Father. His detractors, who knew full well what he
was saying, became so enraged that they took Stephen out
of the city and stoned him to death (Acts 7:54-60). Stephen's
attackers could not bring themselves to accept the fact that
they had become the enemies of God, but they had, due
to their unbelief. Had it not been for the secret hidden in
the mind of God, known as the Mystery, the judgment of
God would have fallen at that time on Israel and the nations in the form of the Tribulation. But God in His infinite
knowledge instead ushered in the Age of Grace. Once He
completes His plans and purpose for the Church and we
are caught away, God will pick up right where He left off at
the stoning of Stephen.

That is the day John describes as he witnesses the activity
surrounding the throne of God. Christ is seen *standing* in

the midst of the throne as the central figure Who is about to execute judgment on His enemies. All eyes are upon Him as He prepares to break sequentially the seven seals of the scroll. The day of the vengeance of our God is before John's eyes. Believing Israel has long awaited this day!

> "And I beheld, and, lo, in the midst of the throne and of the four beasts, and in the midst of the elders, stood a Lamb as it had been slain, having seven horns and seven eyes, which are the seven Spirits of God sent forth into all the earth" (Rev. 5:6).

This verse, so rich with symbolism, now turns to give us a further description of the Lamb. It is important to distinguish thoughtfully between the "seven horns" of the Lamb and His "seven eyes." The *horn* in the Word of God invariably speaks of power and authority when used symbolically (Deut. 33:17). The fact that the Lamb has seven horns indicates that Christ has absolute authority over His entire creation to recover what was lost in the Fall, solely on the basis of His shed blood. These horns, these powers and authorities, manifest themselves in the *sevenfold* characteristics of the Spirit. While they were prevalent during the first coming of Christ, they will be even more pronounced in the coming Day of the Lord. They are inseparably tied to the redemption of all things. These will be the operations of the Spirit according to Isaiah: "And there shall come forth a rod out of the stem of Jesse, and a Branch shall grow out of his roots..."

- And the spirit of the LORD shall rest upon Him,
- The spirit of wisdom and understanding,
- The spirit of counsel and might,
- The spirit of knowledge and of the fear of the LORD.

—Isa. 11:1,2

As we learned in earlier chapters, the "seven eyes" of the Lord is a reference to the seven spirits of God who continuously stand before the throne. These are seven angelic beings of the highest order that stand ready to fulfill the will of God at a moment's notice. Zechariah refers to them when he reminds his countrymen not to despise the day of small things, regarding the humble beginnings of the rebuilding of the second temple in Jerusalem: "For they shall rejoice, and shall see the plummet in the hand of Zerubbabel **with those seven; they are the eyes of the LORD**, which run to and fro through the whole earth" (Zech. 4:10).

A NEW SONG

> "And He came and took the book out of the right hand of Him that sat upon the throne. And when He had taken the book, the four beasts and four and twenty elders fell down before the Lamb, having every one of them harps, and golden vials full of odors, which are the prayers of saints" (Rev. 5:7,8).

If there was ever a doubt as to whether or not the Lamb was *worthy* to open the sealed scroll, any uncertainty is dispelled when Christ takes the book out of the right hand of the Father. The very action itself demonstrates He has the right to open it and the authority and power to accomplish what is recorded therein. The moment the Son receives the scroll from the Father, the twenty-four elders and the cherubim prostrate themselves in humble adoration before the Lamb because they perceive the significance of what He is about to undertake.

Having already established that the earthly temple was patterned after the heavenly, it should not surprise us that the twenty-four elders, who make up a heavenly priesthood, are playing harps as the drama of redemption is about to unfold. We know, for example, King Hezekiah "set the Levites in the house of the LORD with cymbals, with psalteries, and with harps, according to the commandment of David" (II Chron. 29:25). Music, which is an essential part of worship, filled the temple on the earth as it does in Heaven, as seen here in the Book of Revelation. It prepares the heart for the proclamation of the Word of God.

The priestly character of these heavenly ministers is also demonstrated by the fact that they are each holding golden bowls. This particular passage is a good example of how the best commentary on the Bible is the Bible itself. We are blessed with the convenience of having the symbolism of golden bowls explained for us here in the same passage. Of course, the "gold" speaks of that which is precious, while the odors or the fragrant smell of incense represents the *prayers of the saints.* David said essentially the same thing when he sought the face of God: "Let my prayer be set forth before thee as incense; and the lifting up of my hands as the evening sacrifice" (Psa. 141:2).

But what was the nature of these prayers of the saints? Before we answer this question, it is imperative to bear in mind that God is omniscient—He knows the end from the beginning. The Scriptures emphatically state, "And God *remembered* Noah, and every living thing," (Gen. 8:1), even after they had been in the ark for over a year. Unlike men, God never forgets His promises, nor does He forget the prayers of His people, even though they may span many generations. The prayers of God's chosen people, contained in these golden bowls, while too many to number, revolve around three themes that are prominent throughout Israel's history: 1) deliverance from the hand of the oppressor (Luke 1:71); 2) "Thy kingdom come. Thy will be done in earth, as it is in heaven" (Matt. 6:10); and 3) avenging the blood of Israel's martyrs for their stand for the truth (Rev.

6:9-11). As you can see, the ministry of the priests under the Mosaic Law mirrors that of the angelic priesthood in heaven.

> "And they sung a new song, saying, Thou art worthy to take the book, and to open the seals thereof: for thou wast slain, and hast redeemed us to God by thy blood out of every kindred, and tongue, and people, and nation; And hast made us unto our God kings and priests: and we shall reign on the earth" (Rev. 5:9,10).

Most commentators believe the twenty-four elders who are singing this song of redemption are human—namely the 12 patriarchs and 12 apostles of the Kingdom. But as we saw earlier, this clearly cannot be the case because of the timing. Putting this aside for a moment, there is the claim that only redeemed men could sing this song because the angels are not included in God's plan of redemption. Now, while it is true that angels have never been beneficiaries of redemption, they have always been very interested in it (I Pet. 1:12). Further, please permit me to point out that the four cherubim, which everyone agrees to be a special class of angels, are also said to be singing *along with* the twenty-four elders.

It is our firm conviction that *both* the cherubim and the twenty-four elders are classes of angelic beings that are charged with *special* duties and ministries. If this is true, why would they be singing a song of redemption that doesn't apply to them? Well, it is important to remember that the angels are "all ministering spirits, sent forth to minister for them who shall be heirs of salvation" (Heb. 1:14). Since the pronouns "us" and "we" are referring to the redeemed, this would mean that the cherubim and the twenty-four elders are singing the song of redemption on *behalf* of the redeemed in Israel. A similar occurrence is noted the night the Savior came into the world. You will recall how, after the angel had ministered to the shepherds who were abiding in the field, that there appeared a multitude of the heavenly host praising God, and saying, "Glory to God in the highest, and on earth peace, good will toward men" (Luke 2:14). Obviously this saying didn't apply to them; it was rather said for the benefit of the shepherds to whom they were ministering, and to praise God for His *redemptive* work in the incarnation of His Son. In essence, the Peace-Giver has come! Needless to say, the shepherds would naturally share this wonderful news with their countrymen.

Similarly, the cherubim and the twenty-four elders will be responsible to *teach* this new song to the martyrs of the Tribulation and eventually to all believing Israelites. Although many preachers and teachers these days wouldn't dream of making mention of the "blood" from the pulpit, the phraseology of this new song includes the *blood of Christ* without apology. And to this we say, AMEN!

Remarkably, there are only two times in the Scriptures that the angels are said to sing. The first angelic choir convened *before* sin entered God's creation, "When the morning stars sang together, and all the sons of God shouted for joy" at the laying of the foundation of the earth (Job 38:7). The second occurrence is found here in Revelation Chapter 5, as Christ prepares to *redeem* His creation from every semblance of sin, in the consummation of all things.

This new song was composed to honor and glorify Christ, Who is seen here about to embark upon the final phase of redemption that was initiated through His precious blood at the Cross. With the opening of the seven-sealed scroll, Christ will begin to reclaim what is rightfully His and redeem His own "out of every kindred, and tongue, and people, and nation" in the process. The song also confirms that the conditional promise in time past that Israel was to become a kingdom of priests is about to be fulfilled (Ex. 19:5,6). Israel, and those saved out the nations who are saved through her, will reign with Him on the earth in the coming Millennial Kingdom (Rev. 5:10).

TWO AMAZING DOXOLOGIES

"And I beheld, and I heard the voice of many angels round about the throne and the beasts and the elders: and the number of them was ten thousand times ten thousand, and thousands of thousands; Saying with a loud voice, Worthy is the Lamb that was slain to receive power, and riches, and wisdom, and strength, and honor, and glory, and blessing.

"And every creature which is in heaven, and on the earth, and under the earth, and such as are in the sea, and all that are in them, heard I saying, Blessing, and honor, and glory, and power, be unto Him that sitteth upon the throne, and unto the Lamb for ever and ever" (Rev. 5:11-13).

A doxology is "a hymn or liturgical formula expressive of praise to God."[2] It essentially glorifies God. Perhaps one of the more well-known doxologies we've all sung at one time or another is: *"Praise God, from Whom All Blessings Flow."* It was written by Thomas Ken and first appeared in 1674 in "A Manual of Prayers for the Use of the Scholars of Winchester College." Kenneth W. Osbeck comments that this particular doxology "has done more to teach the doctrine of the Trinity than all the theological books ever written."[3]

Praise God, from whom all blessings flow;
Praise Him, all creatures here below;
Praise Him above, ye heav'nly host;
Praise Father, Son, and Holy Ghost! Amen.

As the Apostle John widens his view of the heavenly scene, he informs us that he saw an innumerable host of angels around the throne of God. When John states that he saw "ten thousand times ten thousand, and thousands of thousands," he isn't affixing an exact number to this heavenly host; instead he wants us to understand it was innumerable. We search the Scriptures, but apparently we do not have a name for a number that even comes close to the number of angelic beings that God created in the beginning (Heb. 12:22). When the angelic host that was present said, "Worthy is the Lamb," John remarks that they spoke with a *loud voice*. The apostle isn't suggesting they were shouting; rather, He wants us to be cognizant of the fact that their sheer number speaking in unison was loud, almost deafening!

Both of these doxologies before us (in Revelation 5) are in anticipation of what is about to transpire on the earth. Although there are some similarities between the first doxology here in Chapter 5 and the one found in Revelation Chapter 4, there are at least two distinct differences.

"Thou art worthy, O Lord, to receive glory and honor and power: for thou hast created all things, and for thy pleasure they are and were created" (Rev. 4:11).

Each of the members of the Godhead was actively involved in creation. God the Father designed and purposed it. The Father then acts, but does so through His Beloved Son Who created all things. The Holy Spirit mysteriously "moved" in the creation process (Gen. 1:2; Psa. 104:30), and then reveals and interprets what was accomplished by the Father and the Son.

The doxology in Revelation 4 points to the fact that the Father, manifested in the person of Christ, is the Creator and Sustainer of all things; therefore, the Father is worthy to be worshipped. He is to receive glory, honor and power for His handiwork in creation. The bee, for example, as it darts from flower to flower, has a built in GPS system which allows it to return to the flowers in the order it discovered them, while at the same time calculating the shortest route in the process. This is one of a multitude of examples of design in nature, design which can be traced back to the Father Who is the Designer of all things.

> "Worthy is the Lamb that was slain to receive power, and riches, and wisdom, and strength, and honor, and glory, and blessing" (Rev. 5:12).

The scene now turns to God the Son in Revelation 5 as the host of heaven praises and glorifies Him for His redemptive work, as this doxology clearly conveys. When Christ came into the world, He came to do the will of the Father. He was born into poverty and suffered unspeakable atrocities at the hands of evil men. As He hung there that day on the Cross, the weight of the sins of the world crushed the life out of Him, so that those who place their faith in Him might wear the garments of salvation.

Because of what the Lamb of God accomplished for the redeemed, He is worthy of praise and adoration, for in Him we have life and life abundantly. Our eternal life is dependent upon Christ's death, burial, and resurrection. It's little wonder that the myriad angels of heaven, who have longed to look into these things, could not contain themselves. They joyfully give praise of glory, honor, and power to the One Who was slain, and adding riches, wisdom, strength, and blessing that's justly due Him. When we pause a moment to ponder these four additional crowning praises, we realize that the Lamb is indeed worthy to receive them for what He endured on behalf of Israel, and for us as well, as members of His Body.

"And every creature which is in heaven, and on the
earth, and under the earth, and such as are in the sea,
and all that are in them, heard I saying, Blessing, and
honor, and glory, and power, be unto Him that sitteth
upon the throne, and unto the Lamb for ever and ever"
(Rev. 5:13).

The second doxology of Revelation 5 broadens the scope of
things considerably. We have always emphasized from the
Scriptures that there is only **one** God Who eternally exists
in three Persons; Father, Son, and Holy Spirit. Each of the
Members of the Godhead is co-equal and co-eternal, and of
the same mind and purpose. While this goes far beyond our
comprehension, it is nevertheless true and we accept this
truth by faith. With this mind, this awe-inspiring doxology
resounds throughout the whole universe. It gives glory,
honor, and praise to *both* the Father and the Son. According
to the Spirit, Who never speaks of Himself (John 16:13-15),
they are worshipped here as One, as Creator and Redeemer.

It isn't difficult to surmise that John was probably overwhelmed by all the things that unfolded before his eyes. To
add to his amazement, he heard, "every creature in heaven,
and on the earth, and under the earth, and such as are in
the sea, and all that are in them" saying, "Blessing, and
honor, and glory, and power, be unto Him that sitteth upon
the throne, and unto the Lamb for ever and ever."

In all likelihood, this otherwise universal adoration will
not be coming from evil, unrighteous men in these various
realms. After all, these are the very ones *from* whom the
creation will be redeemed. However, at the Great White
Throne Judgment, they will appear before a holy and righteous God and at the name of Jesus, every knee will bow and
every tongue will acknowledge that Jesus Christ is Lord, to
the glory of God the Father (Phil. 2:9-11). The theological
term for this is *universal subjugation*.

So it is the righteous and the angels in all these regions who will join in universal praise of the Father and the Son for what They accomplished in creation and redemption. It is interesting that, as nature itself is about to be delivered from the bondage of corruption, it too joins in this praise and adoration of the Father and Son. Whether you take the roaring of the sea and the distinct sounds of the animal creation happening in unison to be literal or as a figure of speech, there are two Psalms that support what John experienced firsthand at the throne of God. The point is that God is worthy to be praised!

> "Let the sea roar, and the fullness thereof; the world, and they that dwell therein. Let the floods clap their hands: let the hills be joyful together before the LORD; for He cometh to judge the earth: with righteousness shall He judge the world, and the people with equity" (Psa. 98:7-9).

> "Praise the LORD from the earth, ye dragons, and all deeps: Fire, and hail; snow, and vapors; stormy wind fulfilling His Word: Mountains, and all hills; fruitful trees, and all cedars: Beasts, and all cattle; creeping things, and flying fowl" (Psa. 148:7-10).

The Jewish believers who make up the seven churches in Asia will surely be consoled when they read Chapters 4 and 5 of the Apocalypse. In the midst of the turmoil that they will experience in that day, it will be reassuring for them to know that God is sovereign and in control of all things, as these two chapters so beautifully affirm. They will rejoice that the Lamb is worthy to open the sealed scroll and execute judgment on their enemies, as we will see in the chapters that follow.

> "And the four beasts said, Amen. And the four and twenty elders fell down and worshipped Him that liveth for ever and ever" (Rev. 5:14).

What a fitting close to what has transpired! The cherubim respond to the universal glorification of God, saying, "Amen!" That is to say, "So be it!" Simultaneously, the twenty-four elders fall before the throne and worship the Lord God Almighty as we are reminded by the Spirit, through the written Word, that He is eternal. What a scene!

Now we have come to the hour of reckoning! Who will be able to withstand the fierceness of His wrath?

9

The Four Horsemen of the Apocalypse

"And I saw when the Lamb opened one of the seals, and I heard, as it were the noise of thunder, one of the four beasts saying, Come and see."

—*Revelation 6:1*

As we have seen, only the Lamb is worthy to open the book that was sealed with seven seals. This book contains the judgments of the coming Tribulation. A cursory reading of the Book of Revelation will reveal that there are *three* primary sets of judgments that await the world: Seven Seals, out of which flow the Seven Trumpets, from which come the Seven Bowls. Each subsequent set of these judgments will be more severe as the Tribulation proceeds. There is also another set of judgments called the Seven Thunders (Rev. 10:3,4). They are apparently so horrific that John was instructed to seal up those things that were spoken by these seven angels.

Some find it hard to believe that a loving God would judge the world. It is true that God is a God of love. In fact, He loves us so deeply that He sent His only begotten Son to die for our sins. You see, the judgment of God fell on Christ so that we might be delivered from God's wrath. However, if the sinner rejects the Sin-Bearer, then he must suffer the consequences of his rejection. As Pastor Cornelius Stam always said, "Any infraction against God's infinite holiness demands an infinite penalty." While man has a propensity to condone sin, God cannot! We must never blame God for what man has brought upon himself. Man is simply going to reap what he has sown.

Having established that these judgments are going to come from the throne of God, the scene now shifts back to the earth where these events will actually transpire. When the Lamb opened the first seal, John heard, as it were, "the noise of thunder." As lightning and thunder precede a storm, the "thunder" here marks the *beginning* of the approaching storms of the Tribulation. This is immediately followed by one of the four beasts saying to the apostle, "Come and see!" These four beasts or living creatures are charged with a solemn task. As we noted in the last chapter, the prophet Ezekiel identifies them as the four cherubs that are stationed in close proximity to the throne of God, and serve as protectors of God's holiness (Ezek. 1:5-14; 10:14,15 cf. Rev. 4:6-8). It is these guardians of His holiness that announce the four horsemen of the Apocalypse.

The dreadful events of Revelation Chapter 6 correspond perfectly with the Olivet Discourse, delivered by our Lord to His disciples in Matthew 24. The Lord predicted the following:

Matthew 24

1. "Take heed that no man deceive you. For many shall come in my name, saying, I am Christ; and shall deceive many" (Matt. 24:4,5).

2. "And ye shall hear of wars and rumors of wars....For nation shall rise against nation, and kingdom against kingdom" (Matt. 24:6,7).

Revelation 6

1. The rider of the white horse is the Antichrist who deceives the world (Rev. 6:2 cf. 13:12-18).

2. The rider of the red horse is given power "to take peace from the earth," which results in world wars (Rev. 6:4).

Matthew 24	**Revelation 6**
3. The Lord adds, "And there shall be famines" (Matt. 24:7).	3. The rider of the black horse introduces worldwide famine (Rev. 6:5,6).
4. "Pestilences" or blood diseases will run rampant in that day (Matt. 24:7,9).	4. The rider of the pale (the color of sickness) horse will "kill...with death" (Rev. 6:8).
5. "Then shall they deliver you up to be afflicted, and shall kill you" (Matt. 24:9).	5. After the fifth seal was opened, John "saw under the altar the souls of them that were slain" (Rev. 6:9).
6. We also learn there will be "earthquakes in divers places" (Matt. 24:7).	6. John beheld when the sixth seal was opened that "there was a great earthquake" (Rev. 6:12).

According to the chronology of the prophetic Scriptures, the foregoing events will come to pass during the *first part* of the Tribulation. As a matter of fact, when the Lord concluded this portion of the discourse, He said, "All these are the beginning of sorrows" (Matt. 24:8). Incredible! In other words, this is just the beginning; the worst is yet to come. I don't know about you, but I think we should get down on our knees and thank God that we will never drink from "the cup of the wine of the fierceness of His wrath" (Rev. 16:19).

THE FOUR HORSEMEN OF THE APOCALYPSE

FIRST SEAL
The Rider of the White Horse

"And I saw, and behold a white horse: and he that sat on him had a bow; and a crown was given unto him: and he went forth conquering, and to conquer" (Rev. 6:2).

The first horseman of the Apocalypse is riding a *white* horse. Of course this speaks of dignity or rank. The Napoleons and Washingtons of this world have always been the ones out on the point, riding a white horse as they led their armies into battle. In the Book of Revelation, it is essential to identify the rider of this particular horse, since there are two such riders of white horses found in the record (Rev. 6:2 cf. 19:11-13).

Although some have concluded that the first horseman of the Apocalypse is Christ, they are diametrically incorrect. There is little question that the rider of this horse is none other than the Antichrist. You will note that a crown will be given to him. This is not the kingly crown (the royal diadem) that the King of kings is said to wear. Instead, it is the *stephanos*, the victor's crown that was worn as a symbol of honor in biblical times. This crown being given to the man of sin points to the fact that Satan grants him the authority to go forth and conquer (Rev. 13:4). Needless to say, no one gives Christ authority; He's God, and the very embodiment of authority!

The Antichrist rides onto the world stage at the beginning of the day of the Lord to go "forth conquering, and to conquer." Although we must not underestimate his military prowess, he will primarily conquer through the means of *deception* initially (II Thes. 2:8-10; Rev. 13:11-14). The prefix *anti* means against and/or instead of. Both are true of this future dictator. He poses as the Messiah, but opposes Christ by trying to kill all who name His name. The Antichrist will have a winsome personality that the world will find irresistible. He will have the charisma of JFK, the intelligence and leadership abilities of Winston Churchill, the wit of Mark Twain, the communication skills of Ronald Reagan, and the knowledge of foreign affairs of Henry Kissinger. The prophet Daniel says of him,

> "And the king shall do according to his will; and he shall exalt himself, and magnify himself above every god, and shall speak marvelous things against the God of gods, and shall prosper till the indignation be accomplished: for that that is determined shall be done. Neither shall he regard the God of his fathers, nor the desire of women, nor regard any god: for he shall magnify himself above all" (Dan. 11:36,37).

Here the prophet Daniel gives us a biographical sketch of the Antichrist. As we know, the Tribulation is said to open with wars and rumors of wars (Matt. 24:6). It will be a period of unparalleled iniquity or lawlessness (Matt. 24:21; Mark 13:19). Like Hitler, the Antichrist will take full advantage of the times. In fact, the prevailing culture will provide the platform for him to prosper politically and become a household name overnight.

During the forty days in which Christ was tempted, you will recall that the devil took our Lord up into a high mountain and "showed unto Him all the kingdoms of the world in a moment of time. And the devil said unto Him, All this power will I give thee, and the glory of them: for that is delivered unto me; and to whomsoever I will I give it. If thou therefore wilt worship me, all shall be thine. And Jesus answered and said unto him, Get thee behind me, Satan: for it is written, Thou shalt worship the Lord thy God, and Him only shalt thou serve" (Luke 4:5-8).

Notice that the world lies in the lap of the evil one. The devil gained authority over mankind when Adam fell. Satan rightfully claims full ownership and control of the kingdoms of this world and, in this passage, he offers them to Christ. Of course, our Lord exposed the devil's desire to overthrow the plans and purpose of God by quoting the Scriptures. But the Antichrist, whose coming is after the working of Satan, will gladly *receive* power over the nations from the dragon (Rev. 13:1,2,7) who is Satan (Rev. 12:9). While we know that the Antichrist will be a ruthless dictator who opposes the righteous ways of God, he will begin his reign of terror as a man of *peace*, and the world will be predisposed to accept peace at any price.

Having control of the kingdoms of this world, the Antichrist negotiates a peaceful solution for those nations that are at war with one another. Eventually, he forms an alliance with these nations which serves as his seat of authority (Rev. 13:2 cf. 17:9-13). Simultaneously, the Antichrist strikes a treaty with the nation Israel, which allows her to re-establish the temple and the Old Testament sacrificial system. This brings *peace* to the Middle East.

> "And he [the man of sin] shall confirm the covenant with many for one week [7 years]: and in the midst of the week [middle of the Tribulation] he shall cause the sacrifice and the oblation to cease, and for the overspreading of abominations he shall make it desolate, even until the consummation" (Dan. 9:27).

We believe the Antichrist will seek to *conceal* his identity for as long as possible at the beginning of the Tribulation. In other words, he would never be so foolish as to say publicly, "I have come to deceive and rob the nations of their autonomy." This isn't how deception works. Notice that Daniel states: "He shall confirm the covenant with *many* for one week." This dynamic impostor will establish this peace agreement with "many" in Israel, but *not all*. While he may *deceive* the religious leaders and their followers as to his true identity, apparently *some* in Israel will suspect that he has evil intentions.

The initial, ostensible agenda of the Antichrist will be to bring peace to the world. As this false sense of *security* sweeps around the globe, the world will wonder after the beast, saying, "Who is like unto the beast?" (Rev. 13:4). But "when they shall say, Peace and safety; then sudden destruction cometh upon them, as travail upon a woman with child; and they shall not escape" (I Thes. 5:3). More so than ever before in history, it will be like hell on earth with the wrath of God raining down from heaven and the military machine of the Antichrist crushing anyone or any nation that stands in his path.

> "But in his estate shall he honor the God of forces: and a god whom his fathers knew not shall he honor with gold, and silver, and with precious stones, and pleasant things" (Dan. 11:38).

The Antichrist will use his wealth not only to fund his lavish lifestyle, but also to honor the god of forces. The word *forces* is the Hebrew term *ma'owz* or "fortresses." Satan is the god of fortresses or war. Anyone who has fought in a war will tell you that war is nothing more than confusion, and Satan is the author of it. The general who leads the forces of evil into battle in the coming day of the Lord is indisputably the Antichrist. His military prowess will make the remarkable accomplishments of Alexander the Great look insignificant. He is the rider on the white horse who goes forth to *conquer* (Rev. 6:2). And the main objective of this diabolical leader will be to do battle with the saints and destroy the nation Israel. It's no wonder that the souls of the *martyrs* cry out to the Father, "How long, O Lord, holy and true, dost thou not judge and avenge our blood on them that dwell on the earth?" (Rev. 6:10).

Daniel also informs us that "Neither shall he regard the God of his fathers" (Dan. 11:37). The phrase "God of his fathers" is uniquely Hebrew. The "fathers" is a reference to the patriarchs, namely Abraham, Isaac, and Jacob. For example, upon receiving the decree from King Artaxerxes that Israel could return to the land with the gold and silver vessels of the temple, Ezra offered a prayer of thanksgiving:

> "Blessed be the LORD God of our fathers, which hath put such a thing as this in the king's heart, to beautify the house of the LORD which is in Jerusalem" (Ezra 7:27).

In relation to the Antichrist, he will have little or no regard for "the God of his fathers." He'll have absolutely no desire whatsoever to know Him or worship Him as his predecessors did before him. However, the phrase does clearly indicate that he will be a *Jew*, even though he'll seek to disassociate himself from the Hebrew fathers and what God promised to them. Then Daniel adds, "nor the desire of women" (Dan. 11:37). This phrase can be taken to mean either the Antichrist won't desire women, or women will desire him but he'll be *oblivious* to their advances. In either case, Daniel's point is this: the Antichrist will be so self-absorbed that he'll be more than content to remain *single* or engage in homosexual relationships.

SECOND SEAL
The Rider of the Red Horse

> "And when He had opened the second seal, I heard the second beast say, Come and see. And there went out another horse that was red: and power was given to him that sat thereon to take peace from the earth, and that they should kill one another: and there was given unto him a great sword" (Rev. 6:3,4).

The first horseman will be the very embodiment of evil, but the three horsemen that follow thereafter are demonic beings. With the restraining force of the Body of Christ removed from the earth at the Rapture, God will allow evil to be unleashed upon the world as a form of judgment (II Thes.

2:7-9). This is not the first time God has used this instrument to accomplish His will. When the plagues fell upon the Egyptians, who refused to release Israel from bondage, God permitted evil angels to enter Egypt with catastrophic results. The Psalmist recounts,

> "How He had wrought His signs in Egypt, and His wonders in the field of Zoan...He cast upon them the fierceness of His anger, wrath, and indignation, and trouble, by sending evil angels among them" (Psa. 78:43,49).

This particular judgment was limited to the land of Egypt; however, that which is to come will be far more sweeping and menacing, for these infernal creatures will be allowed to prey upon mankind for years. Since the beginning, men have had a fascination with the spirit world, but what they are about to witness will cause the mightiest of them to tremble in fear.

The second horseman of the Apocalypse appears on the horizon of Jacob's Trouble riding a *red* horse, the color of blood. In that day, the blood of God's enemies will run like a river through the streets of the world. This fallen, demonic being is given power "to take peace from the earth, and that they should kill one another: and there was given unto him a great sword." The opposite of peace is war.

Ever since the dawn of civilization, there have been wars and rumors of wars, but most of these conflicts were isolated to one or two parts of the world. With a flash of the sword, peace will become a casualty of this horseman. A sword is an instrument of death; a *great* sword is an instrument of genocide. With the present-day weapons of mass destruction, one shudders to think what "a great sword" might represent and what lies ahead. The next great conflict is going to be global in nature.

THIRD SEAL
The Rider of the Black Horse

"And when He had opened the third seal, I heard
the third beast say, Come and see. And I beheld, and
lo a black horse; and he that sat on him had a pair of
balances in his hand. And I heard a voice in the midst
of the four beasts say, A measure of wheat for a penny,
and three measures of barley for a penny; and see thou
hurt not the oil and the wine" (Rev. 6:5,6).

The third horseman of the Apocalypse gallops across the
nations of the world spreading famine. He is said to be
riding a *black* horse, which is the color of grief and sorrow
(Lam. 5:10). It has been correctly said that this will be "a
time of famine when life will be reduced to the barest neces-
sities; for famine is almost always the aftermath of war."[1]

In this horseman's hand is a pair of balances to determine the price of equivalents. During the future Tribulation, *inflation* will spiral out of control; this, coupled with
a shortage of food, will cause a measure of wheat to cost
a penny. Here we must pause for a moment to define our
terms so we can more fully comprehend what is being said.
The "penny" is the Greek *denarion*. In biblical times, the
denarion was a day's wages (Matt. 20:1-16). A "measure,"
on the other hand, was about a quart of wheat or enough
food for approximately one day. With this in mind, it will
take a full day's wages to provide two or three meals con-
sisting only of grain. Some will purchase three measures
of barley to extend their daily provisions; although cheaper
than wheat, it is far less nourishing.

Interestingly, the contrast under this judgment is between
rich and poor. Apparently the middle class of the nations
will be nearly nonexistent at that day. As the poor wonder
where their next meal is coming from, the commodities of

the rich, oil and wine, are left untouched by this worker of evil. These will be perks for those seduced by the riches of the Antichrist. The seat of his kingdom will be Babylon, which is destined to become one of the future wonders of the world, just as it was among the seven wonders of the ancient world. It will be a den of iniquity that will perish in one day under the seventh bowl judgment (Rev. 18:1-19).

Immediately following this troubling event, another life-threatening hardship awaits those of the household of faith. In the middle of the Tribulation, the false prophet, who deceives the world to worship the Antichrist, will require "all, both small and great, rich and poor, free and bond, to receive a mark in their right hand, or in their foreheads: And that no man might buy or sell, save he that had the mark, or the name of the beast, or the number of his name" (Rev. 13:16,17). Just when the believers of that day think things can't get any worst, they do!

Apparently food and drink will be plentiful by the mid-point of the Tribulation, *if* you receive the mark of the beast. But those who do so will be eternally damned with no hope of exoneration. Since this isn't an option for those who have placed their faith in Christ, they will turn to God for deliverance. On the wings of eagles, He will sweep them into the wilderness, as He did in time past, and provide for their every need in fulfillment of the Lord's Prayer (Matt. 6:9-13 cf. Rev. 12:14). As we are going to see, it will be necessary for God to make this provision for 3½ years.

FOURTH SEAL
The Rider of the Pale Horse

"And when he had opened the fourth seal, I heard the voice of the fourth beast say, Come and see. And I looked, and behold a pale horse: and his name that sat

on him was Death, and Hell [Gr. *Hades*] followed with
him. And power was given unto them over the fourth
part of the earth, to kill with sword, and with hunger,
and with death, and with the beasts of the earth" (Rev.
6:7,8).

The scene described here is the most chilling of all up
to this point. The fourth horseman of the Apocalypse is
named *Death*, and the evil companion following him is
Hades. Normally in the Scriptures, death is referred to as a
circumstance and *hades* as a place located in the lower parts
of the earth (Isa. 14:15). In the above passage, however,
Death is the death angel, and hell, the angel Hades. It
is important to note the *personal* pronouns (his, him, and
them) that are used in regard to these two emissaries of
Satan. They are mentioned a second time in the Book of
Revelation when they are cast into the Lake of Fire at the
consummation of all things (Rev. 20:14). In every case, God
will ultimately destroy His enemies.

Perhaps we need to pause again for a moment to clarify
our terms. Many times, the reference to the term *hell* in
our English New Testaments is actually *hades* in the Greek.
Since it is impossible to translate accurately from one language to another word-for-word, we must consult the original language at times to arrive at the proper sense. In
view of the fact that we don't have an English word for
hades, the translators chose to use the word *hell* for want
of a better term. It is therefore extremely important to distinguish between the English word *hell*, based on the Greek
term *hades*, and the English word *hell*, based on the Greek
term *gehenna*, which is the final Hell and destination of the
unsaved. A good concordance will serve you well if you are
unsure which term is used in the original language.

The *pale* horse upon which Death rides is the ashen color
of a corpse. Death will claim its victims through contagious

diseases such as SARS, blood diseases such as AIDS, famines such as in Somalia, and terrorist attacks such as 9/11. The difference will be that these types of plagues will be *universal*. Even the animal kingdom will be turned against mankind as wild beasts and venomous reptiles prey upon men on an unprecedented scale. When Death lays its icy grip upon the world of unbelievers, Hades will sweep them into the infernal regions below (Luke 16:19-31).

When the unsaved victims of the death angel close their eyes in death, the angel called *Hades* will cast them into the unseen world (Gr. *hades*) located in the center of the earth, where they will suffer in torment, until the consummation of all things (Luke 16:19-31). Without any hope of reprieve, they will remain in *hades* until the Great White Throne Judgment at the end of the Millennial Kingdom (Rev. 20:11-15). All unbelievers of all past ages will stand before God at that day and will be judged according to their ungodly, evil works (Rev. 21:8). This will determine the degree of their punishment in hell (Gr. *gehenna*) for eternity (Mark 9:42-47).

Under the reign of terror of these horsemen, nearly one-fourth of the world's population will perish. William L. Krewson, Professor at Philadelphia Biblical University, states, "Today's world population stands at about 7 billion. To imagine the sudden death of more than 2 billion people—the combined current populations of China and India—is overwhelmingly frightening." If the days of the Tribulation were not shortened, as foretold in the Gospel according to Matthew, all flesh would be destroyed from the face of the earth (Matt. 24:22). This in itself should give us an even greater appreciation of the present Age of Grace in which we live. And to this, all the Lord's people said, "AMEN!"

10

The Wrath of God

"And when He had opened the fifth seal, I saw under the altar the souls of them that were slain for the word of God, and for the testimony which they held: And they cried with a loud voice, saying, How long, O Lord, holy and true, dost thou not judge and avenge our blood on them that dwell on the earth? And white robes were given unto every one of them; and it was said unto them, that they should rest yet for a little season."

—Revelation 6:9-11

FIFTH SEAL
The Avenger of Blood

The opening of this seal sets to rest, once and for all, the unsound teaching of "soul sleep" and annihilationism. The dear saints pictured in this passage may have suffered martyrdom at the hands of evil men, but their souls are seen here in heaven under the altar of God. Hence to be absent from the body is to be present with the Lord. While these Kingdom saints appear in heaven, this is only a temporary residence, seeing as how they have an earthly hope and calling. Consequently, they will be numbered with the great armies of heaven that return with Christ at His Second Coming (Rev. 19:11-14).

In the disembodied state, the soul and spirit have some type of corporeal make-up unknown to man. These believers are said to be clothed in white robes and demonstrate all the characteristics of personality, having intellect, emotions, and will. Having paid with their lives for their faith, they inquire of the Lord, "How long, O Lord, holy and true, dost thou not judge and avenge our blood on them that dwell on the earth?" The Lamb will speak to their enemies in His wrath, but these martyred saints are instructed to rest for a little season until the Father's purpose is fulfilled.

These saints won't be guilty of any crimes against humanity. Rather, they will be put to death for their testimony (Luke 21:12-17). As a result, the martyr who gives his or her life in the cause of Christ has a very special place in the heart of God. So that we might have a fuller appreciation that the Lord honors His Word, the Avenger of blood will strike down their enemies and usher these faithful servants, who gave so much, into the blessings of His Kingdom (Isa. 63:2-4 cf. Rev. 19:11-16; 20:4-6).

THE SIXTH SEAL
Signs of the Times

"And I beheld when He had opened the sixth seal, and, lo, there was a great earthquake; and the sun became black as sackcloth of hair, and the moon became as blood; And the stars of heaven fell unto the earth, even as a fig tree casteth her untimely figs, when she is shaken of a mighty wind. And the heaven departed as a scroll when it is rolled together; and every mountain and island were moved out of their places" (Rev. 6:12-14).

As God pours out His wrath, all of creation will be touched. Under the sixth seal, the "mountains" and "islands" are moved off their foundations. "Impossible!" the critic will say. We recently had a small, remarkable demonstration of this very thing earlier this year when a devastating earthquake unexpectedly struck Japan. The 9.0 magnitude quake lasted about six minutes, which probably seemed like an eternity for those who actually experienced it. The earthquake was so powerful that it moved the main island of Japan 8 feet to the east. According to seismologists, it was one of the strongest quakes ever recorded since they began keeping records in 1900. This dramatic shifting of the tectonic plates beneath the Pacific Ocean produced a tsunami that swept over the northern islands of Japan, working death and destruction on an unprecedented scale. It is estimated that 10,000 perished from the quake and tsunami.

But things will become far more intense when the Seventh Bowl is poured out later in the Tribulation. At that time, the mountains and islands will *vanish*. "And there were voices, and thunders, and lightnings; and there was a great earthquake, such as was not since men were upon the earth, so mighty an earthquake, and so great....And every island fled away, and the mountains were **not found**" (Rev. 16:18,20).

Some have concluded that the sun turning black as sackcloth of hair and the moon becoming as blood are the results of man-made disasters. For example, during Desert Storm, Saddam Hussein had his Republican Guard set the Iraqi oil fields ablaze. The black smoke was so thick that it turned daytime into nighttime. The sun appeared to turn black. But we must bear in mind that the coming Tribulation is no longer man's day, but the day of God's wrath. These are supernatural events from the hand of God to warn men to repent or perish. The sun turning black, the moon becoming as blood, and the stars falling from heaven like untimely figs is in fulfillment of Peter's prophecy on the day of Pentecost.

> "And I will show wonders in heaven above, and
> signs in the earth beneath; blood, and fire, and vapor of
> smoke: The sun shall be turned into darkness, and the
> moon into blood, before that great and notable day of
> the Lord come: And it shall come to pass, that whoso-
> ever shall call on the name of the Lord shall be saved"
> (Acts 2:19-21).

We must carefully distinguish between the signs of the times prophesied by Peter and the signs to which our Lord referred that will herald His Second Coming at the close of the Tribulation (Matt. 24:27-30; Luke 21:25-28). The supernatural manifestations in heaven and earth of which Peter speaks in Acts 2, and which the Apostle John confirms here in Revelation Chapter 6, are the *same events*. John simply gives a more detailed account of Peter's prophecy. According to Peter, these frightful wonders will appear *before* the latter part of that notable day of the Lord called the Great Tribulation. This is why John says the stars will fall to the earth like "untimely figs." In short, they are a precursor of that which is to come. These signs here in Revelation 6 serve as a warning to those living in that day that time is short! But what will be the response of those who look up and see these terrible wonders in heaven?

> "And the kings of the earth, and the great men, and
> the rich men, and the chief captains, and the mighty
> men, and every bondman, and every free man, hid
> themselves in the dens and in the rocks of the moun-
> tains; And said to the mountains and rocks, Fall on us,
> and hide us from the face of Him that sitteth on the
> throne, and from the wrath of the Lamb" (Rev. 6:15,16).

Men will cry out for the mountains and rocks to fall on them so as to hide them from the wrath of the Lamb. They will fully understand the source of these judgments, yet they will refuse to repent and turn to God who could deliver them from their misery. According to the Lord's own words, *every* event under the Seal judgments takes place during the *first* three and a half years of the Tribulation period. Again, this is only the *beginning* of sorrows (Matt. 24:4-8 cf. 24:15-22).

"For the great day of His wrath is come; and who shall be able to stand?" John closes the chapter with a great question. Who will be able to endure the wrath of God? This question will be addressed in Volume 2. Before we move on to the next chapter, we want to reiterate that, while there are those who claim that the Olivet Discourse is being fulfilled today, this just isn't the case, as we are going to discover in our search for the truth. We conclude this volume with a fresh approach to this debate which we hope will settle the matter once and for all.

UNDERSTANDING THE TIMES

When it comes to understanding the times in which we are living, the Church today is just about as confused as it can be. The vast majority of believers nowadays are convinced that the catastrophic events foretold by our Lord in the Olivet Discourse are unfolding before our very eyes (Matt. 24:3-8). These, they say, "are the beginning of sorrows" which precede the Lord's coming.

With this in mind, here's a brief list of recent events they point to as evidence that these are the end times:

- Hurricane Katrina is but one example of the increase in tropical storms in the Gulf of Mexico. The storm hit the Louisiana coast on August 29, 2005 leaving 1,800 dead in its aftermath. It was the strongest hurricane ever to strike that part of the country, so strong that the storm surge overwhelmed the levee system, flooding nearly the entire city of New Orleans.

- The news footage of the recent Arizona sandstorm, if you didn't know better, certainly looked like a doomsday event. The sandstorm, which ascended nearly a mile into the atmosphere, eerily moved across the city of Phoenix, bringing everything to a standstill.

- This was followed by a heat wave that gripped nearly the entire country with temperatures exceeding 100 degrees. It was so hot in Oklahoma that a reporter from one of the national news agencies cooked a steak to medium well on the dashboard of his car. That's hot! In Texas, hundreds were driven from their homes as wildfires destroyed thousands of acres.

While all these events were horrible and tragic beyond comprehension, they were not in fulfillment of the things predicted in the Scriptures to occur during the End of Days. They were merely natural disasters that happen in a sin-cursed world. In addition, we must bear in mind that, according to the Spirit of God, creation is in a state of decline which oftentimes contributes to these incidents.

> "And, thou, Lord, in the beginning hast laid the foundation of the earth; and the heavens are the works of thine hands: They shall perish; but thou remainest; and they all shall wax old as doth a garment; And as a vesture shalt thou fold them up, and they shall be changed: but thou art the same, and thy years shall not fail" (Heb. 1:10-12).

Most of us probably have garments we feel so comfortable wearing that we overlook the fact that a change is long overdue. Perhaps we've made a few alterations or sewn up the holes in the pockets over the course of time, but eventually we find ourselves faced with the inevitable. It's a fact of life that all things are running down and wearing out. After the Fall, when God pronounced the curse, He sovereignly modified what scientists call "the Second Law of Thermodynamics," to its present state as we understand it today. "This [universal] law states that all systems, if left to themselves, tend to become degraded or disordered."[1] This fundamental tendency is usually called *entropy*.

Thus Scripture and science agree that God's creation is showing signs of gradual deterioration. For example, the ozone layer in the upper atmosphere is slowly decreasing. This is why you find yourself applying sunscreen more frequently, which is now up to 100 SPF, to protect yourself from the harmful ultraviolet rays of the sun. Failure to do so leaves you vulnerable to painful sunburn and even skin cancer. We give thanks that, when we enter the eternal state, God will renovate the present heavens and earth so that they will no longer be subject to decline and ruin due to man's sin (II Pet. 3:12,13).

So the cataclysmic events we have all been witnessing over the past several years are due to the Curse and the aging of the earth. And I think it is fair to say that these occurrences are probably going to become more frequent and severe in the future. However, these events are **not** in fulfillment of the Olivet Discourse, as many claim.

As noted earlier, if we compare the Olivet Discourse with the Seal Judgments here in Revelation Chapter 6, you will find they perfectly match one another (Matt. 24:1-8 cf. Rev. 6:1-17). This is a clear indication that the events of the Olivet Discourse—the wars and rumors of wars, nation rising against nation, famines, pestilences, and earthquakes—will all take place in the coming Tribulation. In that day, these events will be the direct result of divine intervention—God pouring out His wrath. There will be absolutely no question in the minds of those who fall under these judgments that they are coming from the hand of God

(Rev. 6:15-17). These are the *End Times* the Lord spoke of in the Olivet Discourse that will precede His Second Coming to the earth.

So then, the current turmoil in the Middle East, the famines in Africa, and the flesh-eating disease reported in Europe and America are all products of living in man's day and not the fulfillment of prophecy! We will concede, though, that these things could well be setting the stage for the future Day of the Lord when God will resume His prophetic program, after the Rapture of the Church.

THE TRUE NATURE OF THE LAST DAYS OF GRACE

To have a proper understanding of the times in the Age of Grace, we must narrow our studies to Paul's writings. It is the will of God that every member of the Body of Christ be equipped and prepared to live in light of His coming for the Church. If you were properly equipped with the Word, rightly divided, your faith was not shaken earlier this year by the prediction that the end of the world was going to take place on Saturday, May 21, 2011, at 6 p.m.

We all need to be aware of the following points as we serve and wait.

The Mystery of Iniquity

"For the mystery of iniquity doth already work: only He who now letteth will let, until He be taken out of the way" (II Thes. 2:7).

Shortly after the gospel of the grace of God was given to Paul, Satan set into motion an evil scheme known as the "mystery of iniquity." Satan's intermediate goal is to undermine all forms of God-ordained authority and bring the world to a state of *lawlessness*. As we approach the Lord's coming for us, this unrelenting attack is sure to intensify. Satan has already successfully targeted three areas and the damage has nearly decimated our generation.

The *home* is under siege. God's original plan of authority for the headship of the husband and the role of children, who are commanded to obey their parents, has been pushed aside as old fashioned in favor of one's *rights*. The results have been disastrous, as two out of three marriages now end in divorce. Children rebelliously roam the streets, killing one another, as law enforcement stands helplessly by, its hands tied by a liberal judicial system. When our country lost its innocence in the 1960s, God's chain of command was broken and we have been suffering the consequences ever since.

The *Church*, as well, has fallen victim to the adversary. Years ago, when the town drunk passed a church building where the saints were meeting, he would pause and tip his hat out of respect. Today, he leaves his beer and wine bottles on our doorstep. But perhaps the most troubling trend we are witnessing is a lack of respect for the Word of God. We lament that "praise services" are gradually replacing the sound preaching of the Word. Furthermore, believers are turning from the godly counsel of their pastors to godless psychiatrists and psychologists who do not even understand man's most basic problem. Such a disregard for the authority of the Scriptures must surely grieve the heart of God.

Finally, for generations now, Satan has sought to subvert the authority of *national government*. His most effective weapons of destruction have been corruption, dishonesty, immorality, collusion, and greed. One wonders how much longer things can continue at the present rate with economic collapse, civil wars, starvation, and disease threatening the existence of many nations. The world as we know it is headed on a collision course with the Scriptural reality called the Tribulation, a time which will give new meaning to the word *chaos*.

To a world in utter despair, Satan will introduce the *Great Problem Solver*. As we have seen, the Antichrist will arise from obscurity to become history's most infamous leader. The nations will be mesmerized by his uncanny ability to resolve complex problems and will therefore hastily align themselves with his emerging world empire. For the time being, the Body of Christ is holding back this evil plan of Satan to take over the world, but it is extremely important for us to be aware of it.

Perilous Times

"This know also, that in the last days perilous times shall come. For men shall be lovers of their own selves, covetous, boasters, proud, blasphemers, disobedient to parents, unthankful, unholy, Without natural affection, trucebreakers, false accusers, incontinent, fierce, despisers of those that are good" (II Tim. 3:1-3).

We also need to be conscious of the fact that, prior to the catching away of the Church, "perilous times shall come." These will be exceedingly fierce times that will try men's souls. The dispensation of grace began with the Church being persecuted and it will end with a persecution of those who stand for the truth (II Tim. 3:11,12). Mark these words and mark them well: The greatest threat to Christianity today isn't Rome, but Islam. Islam has absolutely no tolerance whatsoever for the Jew or the Christian, as current world affairs demonstrate. But this too must not be confused with the wrath of God that is to come. Once again, any suffering that the true Church may endure before the Rapture will be at the hands of evil men, not God.

These negative *trends* that Paul foresees will characterize *men* in the last days and must not be confused with miraculous signs. There are *no* signs, miracles, or wonders that will precede the Lord's return for the Body of Christ. There are, however, certain *trends* that will be common among men and, sad to report, will also be true of many believers who live worldly lives. A *trend* conveys the concept of going in a general direction over a period of time. For example, gas prices have been trending upward over the past year. In other words, it's a gradual process and, although there have been momentary price "dips," the overall direction is *up*.

Of the nineteen descriptions that Paul uses to characterize men in the last days, we have selected one from the many to demonstrate our point. The term *incontinent* is defined in the original language as being "without self-control." The sense is that there will be an "anything-goes attitude," whether it pertains to lying, swearing, sex, partying, illicit drugs, binge drinking, etc. Extreme behavior will be the order of the day. But haven't all these trends always been prevalent since the dawn of time? True, but Paul is revealing that they will intensify to a point never before seen in the history of mankind.

Beware!

"Now the Spirit speaketh expressly, that in the latter times some shall depart from the faith, giving heed to seducing spirits, and doctrines of devils" (I Tim. 4:1).

"But evil men and seducers shall wax worse and worse, deceiving, and being deceived" (II Tim. 3:13).

In the last days of grace, there will be two areas for which to be especially watchful in regard to those who minister the Word. Paul warns us that some, but not all, will depart from the faith that was once near and dear to their hearts. They will abandon sound doctrine that was first delivered to us by the Apostle Paul and will instead give heed to seducing spirits. As they teach things that are contrary to Paul's gospel, it will cause a great deal of confusion among the brethren, which is a masterful ploy of Satan, who is the author of confusion. But why would these teachers knowingly depart from the truth? The reasons are many and varied: notoriety for discovery of a so-called new truth, wider acceptance in mainstream Christendom, larger numbers, and other temptations of fleshly, earthly gain.

The level of confusion increases dramatically when we add ministers who *intentionally* deceive the unsuspecting to build a utopian or cult-like ministry. Paul says they have "a form of godliness, but deny the power thereof" (II Tim. 3:5). In a word, they will deny the preaching of the Cross, which is the power of God unto salvation (Rom. 1:16; I Cor. 1:18). Those who come under their spell will have their ears tickled with inspirational messages, but there will be a *deafening silence* when it comes to the deity of Christ, the virgin birth, or Christ's precious blood.

The apostle is clear to all who will listen when he says, "from such turn away." If you fail to do so, you will be swept into what is either their unsound teaching or a web of deception. Beware! Paul's solution to avoid these dangers is really quite simple: "But continue thou in the things which thou hast learned and hast been assured of, knowing of whom thou hast learned them" (II Tim. 3:14). In a nutshell, follow Paul as he followed Christ. A well-rounded understanding of Paul's epistles will be a safeguard against error and will protect you from being misled or succumbing to the clever schemes of men.

In my lifetime, I have personally witnessed an acceleration of the things outlined here by Paul. With these trends in mind, keep looking up, for the Lord may be coming soon! This is why it is so important for our spiritual roots to grow deeply into the fertile soil of the Word, rightly divided. It will insure a better understanding of the times in which we live.

The Gospel

If you are yet outside of Christ, you are in a twofold danger: first, of being left behind to go through the dreaded time called the Tribulation, when men's hearts will fail within them as they witness the wrath of God: second, you are also in peril of dying in your sins with no second chance to be saved in all eternity. We are not going to sugar-coat it for you; you are in danger of the hellfire judgment to come. We want you to know, however, that God loves you and Christ died for your sins. You see, the day Christ died at Calvary, He wasn't dying for His sins, for *He knew no sin*. Instead He was dying for the sins of the world—my sins and your sins. God has made a provision for *all*, but to be a beneficiary of this provision, you must believe that Christ died for you personally and rose again (I Cor. 15:1-4; I Thes. 4:14). Salvation is in a Person, and that Person is the Lord Jesus Christ! He alone can save you from your sins and the judgment to come!

Endnotes

Introduction

1. Charles R. Erdman, D.D., *The Revelation of John, An Exposition*.

Chapter 1

1. Ford C. Ottman, *The Unfolding of the Ages in the Revelation of John*, p. 8, (New York: The Baker & Taylor Co., 1905).

2. Howard F. Vos, *Nelson's New Illustrated Bible Manners & Customs*, (Nashville, TN: Thomas Nelson, Inc., 1999), pp. 602-603.

Chapter 2

1. J. Wilbur Chapman, *Present Day Parables*, (Rio, Wisconsin: AGES Software, Inc., public domain 1900), pp. 94-95.

2. W. Leon Tucker, *Studies in Revelation, An Expositional Commentary*, (Grand Rapids, Michigan: Kregel Publications, 1980), pp. 60-61.

3. John F. Walvoord, *The Revelation of Jesus Christ*, (Chicago: Moody Press, 1966), p. 47.

4. E. W. Bullinger, D.D., *The Apocalypse or The Day of the Lord*, (London: Samuel Bagster & Sons Ltd., 1909).

Chapter 3

1. H. A. Ironside, *Illustrations of Bible Truth*, (Chicago: Moody Press, 1945), pp. 34-35.

2. Clifton Fadiman and André Bernard, General Editors, *Bartlett's Book of Anecdotes*, Revised Edition, (Little, Brown and Company, New York), p. 11.

Chapter 4

1. F. W. Grant, *Numerical Bible: Hebrews to Revelation*, (Loizeaux Brothers, Neptune, New Jersey), p. 342.

2. Robert Brock, *The Seven Churches in the Book of Revelation*, (St. Petersburg, Florida: Right Division Inc., 1979), p. 17.

3. Robert J. Morgan, *Nelson's Complete Book of Stories, Illustrations, & Quotes*, (Nashville, Tennessee: Thomas Nelson Publishers, 2000), p. 77.

Chapter 4 (Cont'd)

4. Usually attributed to John Calvin, 1509-1564 A.D.

5. Author unknown.

Chapter 5

1. Author Unknown.

2. E. W. Bullinger, *Number in Scripture*, (Kregel Publications, Grand Rapids, Michigan), p. 243.

3. For a more comprehensive study on the Book of Life, please see the author's commentary on *Paul's Epistle to the Philippians*, pp. 181,182.

4. Paul D. Gardner, *New International Encyclopedia of Bible Characters: The Complete Who's Who in the Bible*, (Grand Rapids, Michigan: Zondervan, 2001), p. 145.

5. Wayne Hudson, *Many a Tear Has to Fall*, (Padon Press, 2001).

Chapter 6

1. Moody Bible Institute, *Today in the Word*, August 1991, p. 16.

Chapter 7

1. Paul D. Gardner (ed.), *Who's Who in the Bible*, (Grand Rapids, Michigan: Zondervan, 1996), p. 83; see also *Strong's Exhaustive Concordance of the Bible*, OT word no. 7205, derived from OT words nos. 7200 (to see) and 1121 (a son).

2. *Ibid.*, p. 569; see also *Strong's Exhaustive Concordance of the Bible*, OT word no. 1144, derived from OT words nos. 1121 (a son) and 3225 (right hand or side).

3. For a full discussion of this topic, see E. W. Bullinger, *Number in Scripture*, (Grand Rapids, Michigan: Kregel Publications, 1067), pp. 123-125.

4. Joseph A. Seiss, *The Apocalypse: Exposition of the Book of Revelation*, (Grand Rapids, Michigan: Kregel Publications, 1987), p. 107.

Chapter 8

1. Joseph A. Seiss, *The Apocalypse: Exposition of the Book of Revelation*, (Grand Rapids, Michigan: Kregel Publications, 1987), "The Book Is Opened/The Lion Is The Lamb".

Chapter 8 (Cont'd)

2. James Orr (ed.), *International Standard Bible Encyclopedia*, (Grand Rapids, Michigan: Wm. B. Eerdmans Publishing Co., 1939), alphabetical listing.

3. Kenneth W. Osbeck, *Amazing Grace: 366 Inspiring Hymn Stories for Daily Devotions*, (Grand Rapids, Michigan: Kregel Publications, 1990), p. 342.

Chapter 9

1. John F. Walvoord, *The Revelation of Jesus Christ*, (Chicago: Moody Publishers, 1989), p. 129.

2. William L. Krewson, "The Seven Seal Judgments," *Israel My Glory*, Volume 68, May/June 2010 issue, p. 15.

Chapter 10

1. Henry M. Morris, *The Genesis Record*, (Grand Rapids, Michigan: Baker Books, 1976), p. 127.

Selected Bibliography

- Barnes, Albert, *Notes on the New Testament, Revelation*, Baker Book House, Grand Rapids, MI, Reprint, 1981.

- Bullinger, E.W., *The Apocalypse* or *"The Day of the Lord"*, Samuel Bagster & Sons Ltd, London, England, Reprint, 1972.

- Drew, Edward, *Studies in the Book of Revelation*, St. Petersburg, FL, 1953.

- Ellicott, Charles John (Edited By), *Ellicott's Commentary on the Whole Bible*, Volume IV, Zondervan Publishing House, Grand Rapids, MI, Reprint, 1981.

- Fee, Gordon D., *Revelation*, A New Covenant Commentary, Cascade Books, Eugene, OR, 2011.

- Gaebelein, Frank E., *The Expositor's Bible Commentary*, NIV, Volume 12, Zondervan Publishing House, Grand Rapids, MI, 1981.

- Grant, F.W., *Numerical Bible: Hebrews to Revelation*, Loizeaux Brothers, Neptune, NJ, 1932.

- Hastings, Jack D., *Revelation for the Advanced Student*, Printed in the United States of America, 1980.

- Ironside, Harry A., *Lectures on the Book of Revelation*, Loizeaux Brothers, Neptune, NJ, Reprint, 1982.

- Jeremiah, David, *Escape the Coming Night*, Word Publishing, Dallas, TX, 1997.

- Larkin, Clarence, *The Book of Revelation*, Erwin W. Moyer Company, Philadelphia, PA, 1919.

- Lenski, R.C.H., *Commentary on the New Testament, Revelation*, Hendrickson Publishers, USA, 1998.

- McGee, J. Vernon, *Thru the Bible*, Volume V, I Corinthians through Revelation, Thomas Nelson Publishers, Nashville, TN, 1983.

- Morris, Henry M., *The Revelation Record*, A Scientific and Devotional Commentary on the Book of Revelation, Tyndale House Publishers Inc., Wheaton, IL, 1983.

- Newell, William R., *Revelation*, A Complete Commentary, Baker Book House, Grand Rapids, MI, Reprint, 1987.

- Ottman, Ford C., *The Unfolding of the Ages in the Revelation of John*, The Baker & Taylor Company, 1914.

- Raud, Elsa, *The Revelation of Jesus Christ*, Bible Christian Union, Brooklyn, NY, 1969.

- Root, William E., *Comments on Coming Things*, Bible Doctrines Publications, Grand Rapids, MI, 1992.

- Seiss, J.A., *The Apocalypse*, Zondervan Publishing House, Grand Rapids, MI, The original edition of this work was published in 1900 by Charles C. Cook.

- Tucker, W. Leon, *Studies in Revelation*, An Expositional Commentary, Kregel Publications, Grand Rapids, MI, 1980.

- Walvoord, John F., *The Revelation of Jesus Christ*, A Commentary, Moody Press, Chicago, IL, Reprint, 1980.

- Wiersbe, Warren W., *The Bible Exposition Commentary / New Testament*, Volume 2, Cook Communications Ministries, Colorado Springs, CO, 2001.

The Berean Searchlight

The *Berean Searchlight* is the outgrowth of a small church bulletin containing brief weekly Bible lessons by Pastor C. R. Stam in 1940. Its publication has become the largest and most important function of the *Berean Bible Society*, reaching monthly into every state of the Union and more than 60 foreign countries.

The *Searchlight* includes in its mailing list thousands of ministers, missionaries and other Christian workers. Also, it is on display in the libraries of hundreds of Christian Colleges and Bible Institutes. The purpose of the *Berean Searchlight* is to help believers understand and enjoy the Bible.

**Send for our FREE Bible
Study Magazine today!**

BEREAN BIBLE SOCIETY
PO Box 756
Germantown, WI 53022

www.bereanbiblesociety.org

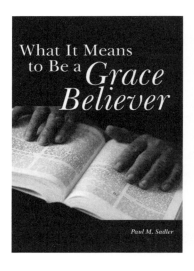

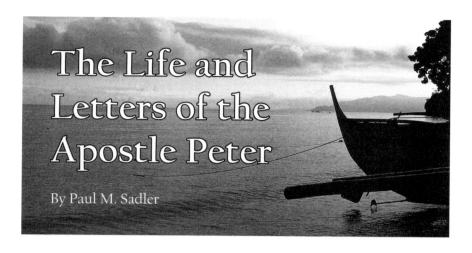

The Life and Letters of the Apostle Peter

By Paul M. Sadler

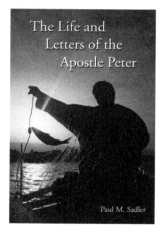

HARDCOVER

250 PAGES

Includes Scripture Index

There is very little written on what are commonly called the *General Epistles* from the standpoint of the Word, rightly divided. This is somewhat understandable to the extent that most of our Grace authors have spent the lion's share of their time addressing Pauline themes. Of course, this has been by design since the commands of Christ for the Church today are found solely in Paul's epistles. Perhaps the time has come to consider the writings of Peter in light of the Pauline revelation.

ORDERS:

Berean Bible Society, PO Box 756, Germantown, WI 53022

www.bereanbiblesociety.org

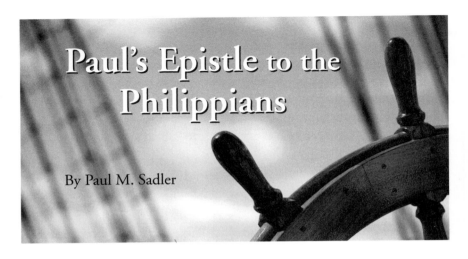

Paul's Epistle to the Philippians

By Paul M. Sadler

HARDCOVER

224 PAGES

BIBLE INDEX

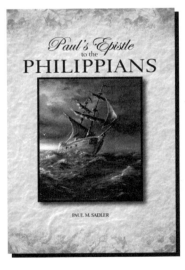

Commentaries on Philippians are as plentiful as mice in a barn. But there are few that approach the narrative on the basis of the distinctive character of Paul's special revelation. Although we have not touched on every jot and tittle in the epistle, we have sought to give a fair and balanced interpretation of the writing.

Orders: *Berean Bible Society*, PO Box 756, Germantown, WI 53022

www.bereanbiblesociety.org